What are people saying about *Relentless Success?*

A potent book about being a world-class performer
by a pro who has lived it. Read this book. Execute
on the insights. Win.

~Robin Sharma, bestselling author
of *The Leader Who Had No Title*

Todd's credentials as a 3x World Series winner, 15
year MLB veteran and the son of an iconic player,
shines through as he shares lessons on persistence,
passion, grit and how to live in the ZONE and how
to succeed.

~Kyle Wilson,
Founder of Jim Rohn International

To become a three-time World Series Champion,
you must be relentless in your pursuit of baseball
success. The same is true in life and Todd
Stottlemyre shows you exactly how to be relentless
and succeed in whatever you do!

~Chris Widener, Author, *The Art of Influence*

What you know influences who you are, which in turn, influences what you do. Permanent change takes place by altering how you think and Todd Stottlemyre presents a clear, concise road map to life-changing excellence.

~John E. Lang,
CEO Pinnacle Development Group

A great book on how to overcome obstacles and win, by a person who lived it!

~Robert Stevanovski,
ACN Co-Founder and Chairman

Relentless Success is one of the most inspiring books you'll ever read. No matter where you find yourself in your career and personal life, this book clearly defines what it takes to think, act and perform like a champion. Take ownership of its contents and you'll discover that there is no circumstance of any kind that can stop you from fulfilling your destiny.

~Larry Raskin,
VP Global Leadership Development of ACN

Todd has lived his life dream and the dream of millions of Little League players who never scratch the surface of that dream. I feel lucky he has shared his system for success and believe anyone who reads it will be a step closer to their dreams.

~ Ron White, USA Memory Champion

Todd Stottlemyre, has created success in every aspect of his life, athletically, personal and business. In Relentless Success Todd has encapsulated how you can create that same success. This book is a must read for anyone for anyone that wants to create their ultimate success in life.

~Gary Varnell, Speaker, Success Coach,
Mentor and author or *Belief*

My friend and championship teammate, Todd Stottlemyre, has been blessed on and off the baseball field. Whether it was pitching and winning playoff games or working sleepless nights to better his businesses, Stott was and is the ultimate competitor physically and mentally. Step in the ring with him and find out why you want him on your side. I'm much better off knowing he's on mine!

~Mark Grace, 15 Year MLB

Relentless Success is a powerful and inspirational message with insight into a real champions life! Todd Stottlemyre a 3x World Series winner shares what it takes to win in life through his personal story! The success principles he shares can be implemented by anyone and will give you the attitude of a champion! I highly recommend this book!

~Tony Cupisz, Co-Founder, ACN

RELENTLESS SUCCESS

9-Point System for Major
League Achievement

TODD STOTTLEMYRE

Made for Success
PUBLISHING

Made for Success Publishing
P.O. Box 1775
Issaquah, WA 98027

Library of Congress Cataloging-in-Publication data

Stottlemyre, Todd,
        Relentless Success:: 9-Point System for Major League Achievement
        p. cm.
        ISBN: 978-1-61339-887-6
        LCCN: 2017905990

To contact the author or publisher please email
service@MadeforSuccess.net or call +1 425 657 0300.
Made for Success Publishing is an imprint of Made for Success, inc.
Printed in the United States of America

CONTENTS

FOREWORD

Right away the title, *Relentless Success*, gets your attention. Relentless is not used often enough as a key to winning. Success is a lot about perseverance through difficulties from beginning to end and onto the next challenge.

This book goes way beyond one catchy word in the title. Todd has developed a 9-point system to success that combines traditional tools with others that emphasize the realities of competing in today's dynamic environment.

The strength of this formula for your success is that each component is explained and combined with Todd's life lessons and experiences. Todd's journey from childhood through professional baseball and business success can be divided into 5 stages.

Stage 1 – Growing up in a loving environment created by outstanding parents and brothers that was filled with learning experiences.

Stage 2 – The heartbreaking illness and death of his brother, Jason. The effect transformed Todd into a prolonged period of sadness, anger and guilt.

Stage 3 – These negative qualities impacted every aspect of his life, especially his athletic efforts. He competed with a reckless abandon with his anger barely in check. In the midst of a game he would often self -destruct if any spark ignited him.

Stage 4 – The road to regaining a positive and productive mental approach towards all parts of his life. The importance of mentors with an excellent example of Harvey Dorfman and his challenge to control his mind.

Stage 5 – Attaining a championship mentality, actions and sustained success in his personal and professional lives. Todd's decision to share his action plan with you and others.

My credentials for recommending *Relentless Success* are the coincidence of getting to know Todd during the last 3 stages of his journey. At first, as an opponent, then as a teammate. As a member of the Oakland A's, we competed against Todd's Toronto Blue Jays from 1988 to 1994. Every time Todd pitched against us, we were aware how hard he was coming after us and how close to the edge he was in terms of maintaining his mental edge. His last year with the Blue Jays (1994), we noticed a more composed pitcher that we felt was explained by more maturity.

Then in 1995 into the 1997 seasons, we benefitted from the pitcher and person in Stage 4 that was regaining control of his mind. He completely became a respectful teammate and leader on and off the field. During this time together I learned a part of how and from whom he was pulling it together.

Once he finished his career with other teams and went into business, I was aware of how well he was succeeding. Stage 5 is well underway. Until I read *Relentless Success*, I did not know all the specifics of the process. I do now and so can you!

Tony LaRussa

INTRODUCTION TO LIVING WORLD CLASS

I WAS BORN the son of a Major League Baseball player. I was not born a major leaguer; that part was up to me. Growing up in Yankee Stadium where my father, Mel Stottlemyre, was a three-time, 20 game winner and a five-time All-Star for the New York Yankees, inspired me to dream big. I wanted to follow in my father's footsteps and play Major League Baseball. My dream became a goal and turned into an obsession. I believed 100% that I was going to live out my dream. I fought against everything that tried to derail me. I never relented to the external pressures or opinions of others. I found that in every small and big success, the process was the same; get in the zone, reach my peak performance and live world-class. These terms became a part of who I am so let me define them for you:

In the Zone

The term "In the Zone" gets thrown around a lot, but for me it is a wholehearted pursuit toward a single, clear goal / task. All distractions are ignored in the zone. Every ounce of mental, physical, emotional, and intellectual strength and energy is 100% dedicated to the task at hand. Any distraction threatening any of these areas must be removed. When you are fully In The Zone, the world is completely silent. Every sense is heightened and tuned towards the task. The Zone is a place of extreme focus.

Peak Performance

Peak Performance is when you are as close to human potential as possible. You are performing at the top of your craft, setting the standards, exceeding expectations, and going beyond what you had believed was possible. My Peak Performance method, covered in this book, is a 9-step process of discipline, principles, and action that will get you to your Peak Performance. When you are at Peak Performance, you experience the immeasurable thrill of feeling and believing that anything you dream of can and will be accomplished.

Living World Class

Living World Class is the light at the end of the tunnel in your life's pursuits. It is living to the highest standard of life that you have set and desired for yourself. It is living at the top of *YOUR* game, not somebody else's. We each have unique dreams and levels of success we want to achieve to be living *OUR* personal world-class lives. Living World Class might look different for each person.

Here's how those three concepts interacted in my successes: First, I learned how to be fully **in the zone**. When I was in the zone, the relentless focus and wholehearted pursuit of my clear vision would allow me to push aside all distractions. With the world around me silenced, I had the discipline and determination needed to work the 9 steps I had developed which empowered me to reach the **peak performance** of my craft. When I was performing at my peak and dedicated to my success, I began **living world class. I** was able to accomplish all that I had set before me and began to make new goals and craft new dreams that would take me even further.

The vision of becoming a Major League Baseball player was so clear that even during the toughest of times, I could "smell the hot dogs in the ballpark". In 1985 my goal became a reality when I was drafted by the Toronto Blue Jays in the first round! People who make *big* goals live *big* lives. You have to first envision what you want and then make it a goal. Actually write it down! You have one life to live; if you want to live it world class, you *HAVE* to start by getting **in the zone.**

It's amazing how life-changing a short amount of time can be when you are fully in the zone. For me, it was 12 consecutive hours of being in the zone with a trusted mentor who permanently changed the trajectory of my life. At the end of our 12 hours I was issued a challenge: For seven days, my mentor challenged me to be aware of my emotions and recognize the challenges that each day brought. I needed to stay in control of my mind and emotions for each challenge I faced. Previously, I had a bad habit of allowing my emotions to control me, but for that one week, to be in my zone I purposed to pay attention to my emotions and reestablish my control over them.

The ultimate test of this life-changing challenge came on a night that began as a celebratory evening with my friend Dave Stewart. His mentorship was so invaluable in both my personal life and my career. Dave was my role-model, mentor, teammate, and friend. We both arrived at the 1994 spring training at the same time, a few days earlier than the start date. Since we had been in contact throughout the off-season and he had quickly become my good friend, I invited him to dinner to celebrate his 37th birthday. I hired a limousine and booked a dinner at a five-star restaurant in Tampa Florida. I wanted to show Dave how much I appreciated him. We got off to a late start that night, not getting to dinner until after 9 p.m. One of my buddies who owned a law firm was also in Tampa that night, so we agreed to meet up after dinner and have a drink. It was a great night; we had a great dinner, and I was spending time with my mentor. We laughed, told stories, and talked a lot about our goals for the upcoming season. We were excited for spring training to start. After Dave and I met my friends for a drink, we jumped back into the limo to head home.

We decided to make one more stop on our way home. A nice bar to have a nightcap and Dave insisted on covering the charge to get in since I had covered the rest of the night to celebrate his birthday. I agreed and said I would go in and get a table while he was getting out arranging to cover the door charge for our group. Right as I was grabbing a table, I felt a tap on my shoulder. I turned to see Dave's friend who informed me that they wouldn't let Dave inside. I headed for the door to see what was going on and Dave was nowhere in sight. As I walked outside, I saw Dave about thirty yards away standing on the sidewalk with three guys standing around him.

"Is everything ok?" I yelled over to Dave as I headed in his direction. He didn't respond. At this point, I knew something wasn't right. As I was walking towards Dave, there were police officers arriving on the scene, it seemed by the dozens. The night went from celebratory to out of control in a matter of seconds.

"Get back!" an officer yelled at me as he cut off my path to Dave.

"I was just getting my buddy and we were leaving" I replied calmly.

"It's too late for him!" the officer shouted in my face, clearly hyped up and overreacting to the situation. He pushed me backward and my hands went up to let him know that I was not there to cause problems. As my hands went up, I was taken down from behind by another officer. I was now lying on the street face down. I had no idea what was going on with Dave. I had several officers on top of me trying to get me in handcuffs. I was face down with my arms outstretched. Then my left arm was ripped behind my back.

"Give us your right arm!" They screamed at me.

The rough pavement burned against my face as they grabbed my hair from behind and slammed my head into the pavement repeatedly. They were completely out of control, acting like they were in a war zone. I stayed calm, able to find the zone, keeping my emotions under control and not reacting with my usual tendency to fight back. I was also protecting my right arm, however, knowing that any damage could harm the way I made a living.

As I tried to push more into the zone and silence the chaos around me, I was jolted by a strong punch to my ribs. The officers had pulled out their metal clubs and were repeatedly beating me on my side trying to get me to roll over. The officers were slamming my forehead against the pavement and taking batting practice on my ribs. I was taking a beating in public on the streets of Tampa! They ripped my right arm behind my back and cuffed me. However, before sitting me in the back of the police car, they took one final blow and slammed my head against the car. I had no idea what was going on, but there I was, after what started out as a perfect night with my mentor, handcuffed in the back of a cop car. My shoulder ached as my pitching arm was tightly cuffed behind my back, warm blood dripping down my face after being smashed into the pavement and the side of car.

"What happened?" I asked the officer in the driver seat.

"I don't know," he replied.

"Why am I in the back of your car?" I continued, my hazy mind catching up to the shock my body was experiencing from the brutality.

"I don't know," he repeated.

Well I didn't know either! I didn't know where Dave was and didn't know why I was in the back of a police car. But I did know that I had received a beating by some cops that were out of control, and that I had chosen not to fight back. Which of course was contrary to my normal mode of operation. A sense of relief washed over me as I realized I had won the ultimate challenge; I stayed in the zone, controlled my emotions and didn't retaliate! The officer driving the car didn't take me to the police station. He took me to a building in the middle of nowhere and locked me in a cage. It looked as if we were in an old school building. The cage was so small I couldn't even stand all the way up, and my elbows were touching either side of the cage while my hands were still tightly cuffed behind me. I felt like an animal being caged and taunted. That's when I saw Dave in the cage next to mine.

"What in the hell happened out there Dave?"

"The guy at the door wouldn't let me in because I didn't want to wear the wristband," Dave said. "He got nasty and threatened me, and then he called the police."

Internally I questioned if all of this could really be over a wrist band. The guy at the door saw us getting out of the limo. Was the guy at the door being a hard ass because he was jealous of Dave's success? Was it because Dave was a massively successful athlete and the guy at the door was taking his shot at stardom? Was he discriminating? I had no idea what triggered it, I just knew there was no violence prior to the police arriving, and yet here we were, locked in cages after taking beating, totally unprovoked.

The Police kept us cuffed in the cages for around four hours. During that time, one after another showed up, about 25 in all. Dave and I sat in our cages watching them all collaborate and "get their stories straight." It was ridiculous and sickening as we listened to the lies they were composing. Officers who hadn't even been a part of the arrest were coming in and spinning a story about how Dave or I had thrown punches at them, even though we didn't resist at all. They then unlocked us from the cages, keeping us cuffed, and transported us to the Tampa Police Department. As they walked us outside, there were cameras everywhere from various national media outlets. They booked us at the station, and we posted bail around 5:30 a.m.

We were both charged with battery on an officer, resisting arrest, and then they added one more charge to Dave, disturbing the peace. We were charged for hitting the police, even though it was really just the opposite! The news media went crazy. They took the police reports as fact and ran the stories making Dave and I look like crazy villains running wild in the streets of Tampa. The only comment that Dave and I were permitted to make to the media was, "No comment." Our case was going to court, and we were coached to say nothing.

I called my parents immediately, to let them know I was ok. I told them that everything on the news was a lie. They trusted me. They knew that every time I made a mistake, I was the first to take full responsibility for my actions. This time, I was letting them know that the media and police department were all lying, and there was nothing we could do about it until the case went to court. But that was one of the main problems; the case was set to go to court in November after the baseball season ended! Basically, that meant that Dave and I were going to be slated as criminals the entire season. "Jailbird! Jailbird! Jailbird!" The taunting chants of the opposing teams' fans still ring through my memory.

The bombardment of slander and our legal situation continually sent me back into the zone, silencing the undeserved jeers and ignorant opinions Dave and I received during that season. I remember warming up in opposing stadiums' bullpens and having their fans chant "jailbird" over and over. It was brutal, but with every challenge, I was building my new mindset. I was constantly challenged to not give my mind over to my circumstances, stay in the zone, and be secure in what I knew to be the truth. Everyone knew how fiery I was on the field while competing, so they all assumed that the news coming out of Tampa was true. They didn't know about my life-changing mentality shift just the week prior. It was a long season with all the distractions. After the 1994 season was cut short, it was time to prepare to go to court.

We were up against the city of Tampa and two dozen police officers who had carefully constructed their stories. It was a jury trial so we were counting on honest citizens to see the truth and decide in our favor. We were up against some serious charges, and if we lost, we could both be facing up to five years in prison. Both Dave and I had our own attorneys, but the case was tried together. The city of Tampa had two attorneys plus the state's District Attorney. It was crazy that the District Attorney was a part of this case. Typically, the District Attorney would be more focused on hardcore criminals rather than a couple of professional athletes, but that shows how seriously the city was looking at our case. My parents and my older brother Mel Jr. came to support me during the trial. I felt bad dragging my family through the mess with me. We hired a private detective to "get the word on the street" inside the police force. We learned that the running joke inside the Tampa police was that when they won the case, they were going to sue Dave and me so they could all buy boats and name them the Blue Jays. The things that came out in the courtroom were unbelievable.

Every officer testified on the stand under oath, but one of the officers was caught in a lie on the stand. The courtroom went wild. The judge immediately called for order and removed the jury from the courtroom before calling all the attorneys to the stand. The judge told our attorneys that we had a case for a mistrial because the officer had committed perjury on the stand. Our attorneys let both Dave and I know that we could walk from this now on a mistrial. We both said "No way!" We were going pursue this case to prove our innocence. We didn't hit any officers; we were caught up in a serious police brutality case. We had been through hell, and we wanted to see this through so the truth could come out. We couldn't win our reputations back on a mistrial.

The trial was tough on my parents and my brother. It was very emotional for them listening to the police tell lie after lie. I stayed calm. I was focused and in control of my mind. I owned it. We spent seven long days in the courtroom. Every day, after leaving the courtroom, a Tampa police car would follow me to the city limits. It was like they were trying to intimidate me. All the attorneys involved in the case made their closing arguments and the judge then dismissed the jury for deliberation. I remember being with my brother and my parents in the hallway while we waited for the jury to make their decision. It was nerve wracking. I knew that we were right, but we were counting on people, like you and me, to make the final decision.

They called us back into the courtroom quickly. The

jury had decided: NOT GUILTY on all counts. Every officer was in the courtroom. It was so satisfying to watch the officers leave the courtroom, one-by-one after the decision. The same people who had beaten us physically on the streets earlier in the year had taken a moral beating in the courtroom. It was over. Dave and I were free, and our names were cleared!

It was crazy how many letters I received over the next couple of months from attorneys who wanted me to sue the City of Tampa and the police department. I never once even gave it a thought. I was tired, and they knew they were wrong. My suing them wasn't going to change anything. It was time to move on with my life and my baseball career, but not without the experiences and lessons learned that I would be applying to the rest of my life.

One week of focusing on staying in the zone and not giving my mind away served me in a real-life situation. It could have had devastating consequences for both Dave and I, had I reacted with my prior habits. My resolve to immediately and relentlessly apply the lessons I've learned from my mentors in baseball, business, and life is what has brought me the successes that I've had. Other challenges came up as the years went on, but my mindset was where it needed to be. When I faced challenges in the future, I learned different lessons from each one, but being mentally in the zone permeated all that I did. I was back in control. The game-changing aspects came from the fact that I applied the lessons immediately during that police brutality case.

Learning the Peak Performance method and learning how to live in the zone is essential. Resolving to commit relentlessly to this system saved my life, career, and future that night. Fully committing to the Peak Performance method will launch you into your dreams and goals as well. You can succeed, and you deserve to live out your dreams to their fullest potential. Yes, there are going to be plenty of obstacles and many things that are out of your control. I am going to help you focus on the things that you *can* control so you can climb to the peak of your success.

CHAPTER 1

STEP 1: SETTING GOALS

THE FIRST KEY to the Peak Performance method is setting goals. Do you remember that childhood feeling of invincibility? When we thought about the future, everything seemed possible. Our dreams were massive, and we were convinced we would not live small lives. That adrenaline of limitless possibilities coursed through my veins every time I roamed Yankee Stadium alongside my dad's team as a kid. Being around some of the greatest baseball players of all time and watching their every move inspired me to dream of following in their footsteps. For me, it wasn't a distant "if" because I was spending my time dreaming alongside the very role models I wanted to one day emulate. My environment fueled my dreams. My brothers and I roamed the field in our Yankee uniforms playing ball, knowing that time was all that separated us from the desires of our hearts. The percentages drastically opposed our dreams, but our childlike faith told us otherwise. The vision of playing Major League Baseball was crystal clear. We could feel the grass and infield dirt of Yankee Stadium under our cleats as the dreams grew in our hearts. Every time my father took the mound, I would watch carefully and think, "Someday, that will be me!"

My desire was birthed and fostered by my environment. My vision was based on my real-life experiences and observations. My belief in the plausibility of my dreams was founded by seeing my father live out that dream. However, I couldn't hide in the shadow of my father forever; I had to do the work and embark on my own journey to become a Major League Baseball player. My childhood environment had set up my desire for what I hoped to accomplish, but accomplishing it was up to me.

I recognize that I was extremely fortunate to live a life where my environment shaped my goals, and I had a front-row view of the detailed reality of exactly what I was hoping to achieve. For you, this process may be reversed. Rather than your environment shaping your goals, your goals may need to shape your environment. Different seasons in life might look different. As I will talk about later in this book, my business success was a season of life where my goals that shaped my environment rather than the other way around.

As we travel through life, some of the goals and dreams we had as children fade away. That is certainly ok. I'm talking about what to do from the here and now and how to keep moving forward. I am a firm believer that when we have thoughts or desires that touch us, that make us stand up and pay attention, that those are reminders of what is possible for us. Too many times people quit before they even get started. I love the famous Zig Ziglar quote, "You don't have to be great to start, but you have to start to be great!" How true is that! Some of us have lost sight of the belief that anything really is possible. Many times, people will quit as soon as moving forward starts to get difficult. Anything worth doing is going to come with challenges, especially when your dreams and goals are BIG. People who think big and do big, ultimately live BIG.

The first step is to get clarity on and solidify your goals. But before you can set goals you must create a mental picture of the desired outcome. It's your time to be childlike again and dream without limitations. What will success look like? What will it feel like? What will your daily life be like? What will your weekly, monthly and yearly schedules look like? How will your family be impacted? How will your life be different from what it is right now? You want to craft a desire that is as detailed as possible, so you have a launching point in articulating your goals. You need to clarify what you are working towards is a life you want, and a life you can handle.

For me, that desire was clear from a very young age because of my environment. I saw my father's life and what his schedule was. I saw the practice schedules and knew the ins and outs of game day. I saw the social life that resulted from the relationships with his teammates' families. I knew when the off seasons were and the intensive training seasons. I had a clear vision of the life that I desired even before I knew the details of what it would take for me to get there or stay there.

Once your desire is clear, it is time to turn your mental picture into a concrete goal. The dream may be a picture of your desire, but the goal is the destination of the future. Let your goals become a must, rather than a maybe. Awaken the champion that lives inside of you. Repositioning your dreams into goals takes the picture and makes it a real destination. It's the difference between dreaming about your next vacation by flipping through a magazine and planning the details once the plane tickets have been purchased. Even if the destination is the same one from your dreaming phase, planning with tickets in hand holds a different weight. You know you will get there no matter what. Your destination is decided. There's still planning to do and details to work out, but the destination is established. When your goal becomes a must, you will find a way to hit that goal. We must attach ourselves to the result in order to set and achieve our goals.

As Tony Robbins says, "We live who we believe we are." If you believe you can accomplish your goal, then you will live as someone capable of accomplishing that goal. If you think you can't succeed, then you won't. I promise you will prove to yourself and everyone else what you believe is possible. If you think your company is going to break records, then you will get your company to the place where it is going to break records. Believing your goals are achievable frees you to think outside the box for solutions.

By choosing a goal and not a dream, you give yourself permission to dedicate time and effort to pursuing that goal. You are willing to take risks once you have decided that what you're reaching for is possible. You might not know the "how" but you will put in the necessary time to discover the "how." I didn't know exactly how I was going to play Major League Baseball and I surely didn't sit down to figure out the percentages of me doing so. I owned my goal, and it became who I was, even before it was accomplished. I grew up knowing I was a future MLB player. In my mind, there was no way it wasn't going to happen. You have control over your belief system. It's yours to own. Do not give it up to smaller thinkers who tell you otherwise.

To live world class, you must fully commit to the Peak Performance method, giving you the ability to overcome great disappointment and continue moving forward towards your goals. No one ever said it was going to be easy to create greatness. Our minds are filled with self-doubt and cluttered with negative thinking. Every time a negative thought comes to your mind, stop yourself and replace it with a positive. I can't tell you how many times I had to do this over my major league career. Imagine the thoughts of facing Cal Ripken Jr, Barry Bonds, Derek Jeter, and other major league greats. I had to have a mindset of "I can do this." You must have that same mindset to reach your peak performance. Let's continue to move our thinking and mindset away from "I can't" and into "I can" and climb the mountain of success together.

Setting a goal is just the beginning step of the Peak Performance method. Being around a positive environment is important, but remember that nothing happens until we get into action. A goal without action is nothing more than a fantasy. Talk is cheap; it's all about doing. As Yoda would say, "There is not try, there is only do." To live to your greatest potential, it takes everything you have. But don't you want it with everything you have? Use that! The bottom line is that you will have to work like your life depends on it. Let's face it; the life you want *does* depend on it. I can tell you that there were many days that I didn't feel like going to practice.

This method is not about what you want to do. It's about what you must do to hit your goals and live out your dreams. During my Major League career, my mantra was very simple, "I am the first one to the ballpark and the last one to leave." With few exceptions, my actions aligned with this declaration. I might not have the most talent, but I was going to outwork my competition. Whenever I took the mound, I always had the mindset that I deserved to win because I knew I had outworked the guy I was facing at the plate. That work ethic and mindset gave me my edge to success. Another person or company may have more talent or a better product, but nothing wins like hard work and a focused game plan.

In his book, *The Five Major Pieces to the Life Puzzle,* Jim Rohn gives the following example:

"A tree does not grow to half its potential size and then say, I guess that will do. A tree will drive its roots as deep as possible. It will soak up as much nourishment as it can, stretch as high and as wide as nature will allow, and then look down as if to remind us of how much each of us could become if we would only do all that we can. Why is it that human beings, surely the most intelligent life form on earth, do not strive to achieve their maximum potential? Why is that we allow ourselves to stop halfway? Why are we not constantly striving to become all that we can be? The reason is simple. We have been given the freedom of choice. In most cases choices is a gift. But when it comes to doing all that we can with our abilities and our opportunities, choice can sometimes be more of a curse than a blessing. All too often we choose to do far less than we could do. We would rather relax under the shade of the growing tree than to emulate its struggle for greatness."

But not *you* and not *now*! Make the commitment to work harder than you have ever worked, dream bigger than you have ever dreamed, and live bigger than you have ever lived. Remember that everything is possible; the impossible is just something that hasn't been done yet. Think about some of the things that we now take for granted that were developed or achieved by big thinkers. Take Roger Bannister, he was the first man to break the four-minute mile in 1954. What was once deemed "impossible" became standard once he achieved that time. Henry Ford created the first affordable automobile in 1910; the famous Ford Model T. Imagine what life would be like for you right now without the automobile. The Wright brothers invented the airplane. It blows my mind how air travel can take you from Los Angeles to New York City in about five hours and people fly every day without thinking of the once "impossible" dream of air flight. Can you imagine how many people told the Wright brothers that they were crazy and that they would never be able to accomplish their dream of air travel? There are miracles all around us of people just like us who have achieved extraordinary dreams because they turned that dream into a goal and decided that it **was** possible.

One of my all-time favorite stories is about Michael

Jordan when he *didn't* make his varsity basketball team as a high school sophomore and had to play on the junior varsity team. It's hard to believe that there were 10 players who made the varsity team over Michael. I'm sure glad that he didn't give up on his dream because of a minor setback. What would the NBA be like today without the career of arguably the greatest player who has ever lived? Michael set the standard on how to measure greatness in basketball.

What setback in your life is holding you back? What would you consider your *junior varsity* season? I had many setbacks that threatened to derail my dream of playing Major League Baseball. One of my mentors once told me, "to have success you must plan your work and then work your plan." Working my plan when setbacks arise helps me not feel stuck. The next step is to make your plan and write your goals down on paper. Writing your goals begins to give them life. It has been proven that people who write down their goals have a much higher chance of success than the people who don't. I have lived by this philosophy my entire life.

Action Plan

Write out up to 3 of your top goals in each of the 8 main categories of life.

	Goal One	Goal Two	Goal Three
Business / Career			
Family			
Financial			
Health / Fitness			
Lifestyle			
Personal Development			
Relationships			
Spiritual			
Other			

Top Goals

Now go through your goals and pick 3 to 5 that will make the biggest impact in your life by achieving them this year.

My Top Goals		
Category	Goal	Reason

Congratulations, you have taken the first step to achieving Peak Performance and Living World Class!

CHAPTER 2

STEP 2: NEW BEHAVIORS

I THINK IT'S safe to assume that if you have picked up this book, you have something in your life that you want to change. The only way to make the Peak Performance method work is by taking what you read and acting on it. That is why Step 2, New Behaviors, is essential to your success. New behaviors become habits that create new skills. If you want to change your life, I guarantee there are new skills that you will need to develop or strengthen. You must identify and prioritize the areas you need to grow and intentionally dedicate time to those skill-building behaviors. This process establishes your fundamentals—the new behaviors that you can build on to develop the big habit changes that are essential to your success.

When you are building your fundamental habits, start small. Find a few smaller new behaviors that will be essential for your end goal, but will give you quick results.

These behaviors are just your first step to behavior changes. They need to be small enough to be easily implemented and maintained. They need to give you quick results because you are re-training your brain to crave this type of change. If you don't see results, you will lose your motivation to change. By making your first step small changes, you start laying the foundation for bigger changes. The little habits developed by small changes will need to be involuntary when it comes time to implement bigger changes.

Being a baseball player with big dreams of reaching the major leagues, I spent countless hours on the field drilling the basics. Practicing the fundamentals and developing skills that were essential to becoming a world-class pitcher. Learning the *small* techniques enabled me to learn the big pitches. Once you have the basics down, the fundamentals of your discipline are ingrained in you, and they become a part of you. Then when someone explains the method behind the new "pitches," you inherently know which small pieces and skills will make up the new "pitch" that you are aiming to perfect. You are confident that you have the tools to succeed; you just need to practice the new behaviors.

Think back to when you were a child, and your parents asked you every day if you brushed your teeth. Now fast-forward to today. You brush your teeth every day in the same routine without any thought. It has become a habit and a good one at that. Habits separate successful people from unsuccessful people. Leadership guru John C. Maxwell was quoted in the book *The Compound Effect*, "You will never change your life until you change something you do daily. The secret to your success is found in your daily routine." New behaviors done consistently over time will produce great habits and great results. The key phrase is *over time*. No one ever made a goal and achieved it overnight. You don't have to have the most talent; you just need the best habits paired with the best work ethic. As Michael Jordan says, "You can practice shooting eight hours a day, but if your technique is wrong, then all you become is very good at shooting the wrong way. Get the fundamentals down and the level of everything you do will rise."

That quote from Michael Jordan reminds me of the days on the half field in spring training doing pitchers' fielding practice. Yes, believe it or not, pitchers work on their fielding every day in spring training. There is a very specific play that we practice thousands of times during spring training. When a ground ball is hit to the first baseman, covering first base becomes the pitcher's responsibility. As a pitcher, you need to understand the foot speed of the hitter to know how quickly to get to the bag. It's not just getting to first base and covering the bag; there is a very specific route that must be taken to produce consistent results. Messing up this play can be very costly to the pitcher and his team, so we practice it thousands of times in spring training. Every time a ball is hit to the right side of the infield the pitcher's first response is to break towards first base. It must become an involuntary reaction. It must be an ingrained habit. Nothing drives a manager crazier than when a pitcher doesn't cover first base on a right infield hit or grounder. It's an easy out when done properly. There is no time for the pitcher to pause; this play is a core part of your identity as a pitcher. The slightest pause can mean a base hit that should have been an easy out. A pitcher with great fielding habits creates great results and a pitcher with poor fielding habits creates poor results.

Great habits create superior results. Initially, new behaviors take considerable energy and will power as you're creating your new normal. However, well-established good habits are energy feeders rather than energy drainers. In other words, your new habits will fully reimburse you with interest for whatever they seem to drain in their infancy. Once your new behaviors are routine, you will be well on your way to becoming a peak performer who is living world class. Wanting what the high achievers have requires doing what the high achievers do.

Jim Rohn says, "Success is nothing more than a few simple disciplines, practiced every day; while failure is simply a few errors in judgment, repeated every day. It is the cumulative weight of our disciplines and our judgments that lead us to either fortune or failure." Everyone can create great habits. It doesn't take any special talent to create great habits and great routines. Success is waiting for every one of us. Ordinary people all over the world have created extraordinary results and lives because of their habits. Creating a new habit in one part of your life leads you to develop great habits in other parts of your life. Success breeds success and great habits breed other great habits.

We need to measure what's important to us, look at our goals, and determine what habits we want and need in our lives. You can't manage what you don't measure. First, we create our habits and then our habits create us. What are your current habits creating you to be? What will your new behaviors create you to be? Look in the mirror. Do you like what your habits have done to you? Even if you are pretty proud of the person you are right now, dig down to the areas that still need improvement. This could be looking at areas of weakness, or even looking at your strengths. Sometimes strengthening the things that you already naturally succeed in can push you into a new realm of success. By refining your strengths, you can cover your weaknesses long enough to get your life to a place where you have more space to give your weaknesses the time and attention they need. I experienced this process on a physical level with various injuries in my career. I had to strengthen the parts of my body that could compensate for my weaknesses. I had to develop new behaviors that would play to my strengths and relieve my weaknesses from the pressure of performing at the top level for that season.

Whether you determine you are in a season of playing to your strengths or strengthening your weaknesses, you will need to develop new behaviors. Peak performers are born when they commit to life-changing habits. Habits – good and bad – are developed by consistency. If you have consistent bad habits that you are hoping to break, you will need to replace them with consistent new behaviors that are good. You already know this, but actually doing it is the hard part.

Start with something small and trackable that will give you quick results. Give yourself two weeks. Week one, go about your normal habits and keep a small notepad with you and jot down every time you have a thought relating to your goals. Week two, implement a few small changes that you think will give quick results and continue to track your thoughts. For example, if your goal is to live a healthier lifestyle but you're addicted to the snooze button, allergic to exercise, and never seem to have enough time in the morning for breakfast, here's an idea of what starting small would look like:

Goals for a healthier lifestyle:

1. Become a morning person

2. Eat 3 full nutritious meals a day

3. Exercise 3 days a week

Week one notes:

- Day 1 - "It's only 10 AM and I am already drained, exhausted, and super hungry. Can't wait for my lunch break!"

- Day 2 – "Hit snooze for 30 minutes this AM. I always feel like such a lazy person when I do that. Ran out the door on time, but felt super rushed through everything as usual. I really need to work on this."

First Step - New Behaviors for week two:

1. Get out of bed 15 minutes earlier

2. Eat breakfast (*doesn't even have to be healthy yet*)

3. Park in the furthest spot away from every building I go into

Week two notes:

- Day 1 – "Didn't get hungry today until right before lunch! Was running late for my meeting after stopping by the grocery store, had to jog back to my car…it wasn't that bad, and I still made the meeting on time!"

- Day 2 – "Hit snooze today, but still got out of bed 10 minutes earlier than my usual last week. I made sure to grab a banana and protein bar on my way out the door, so I still got a small breakfast! Parked further away from the office than usual."

When you get to the end of week two, you can see how the small changes made an impact. You didn't start trying to achieve every part of every goal right away because this can quickly lead to burnout, but you started shifting your behaviors towards consistently pursuing your big goals. You are re-training yourself in the fundamental elements of your big goals. You start to feel like your goals are possible; like you are the type of person who can change and achieve the things you're pursuing. At the end of week two you're now disciplining yourself to wake up and prioritize breakfast, so now it will be easier to make a healthy breakfast with enough time to sit and enjoy a cup of coffee as well. You may not hit the gym 3 times in week 2 since that wasn't your goal for the week, but you walked more this week than you did the first week and that is a healthy habit. Eventually, you may be waking up early enough to eat a healthy breakfast *and* hit the gym before work. You may become that morning person who always takes the stairs, isn't afraid of the back of the parking lot, and is used to being healthy in every aspect of life. The small steps build up the foundation for your future success.

Maybe you know yourself well enough to know you need to strike while the iron is hot when you have new goals and passions. Maybe instead of two weeks, you need to shorten this process to two or four days. The timing is not as important as the process – small trackable changes that will produce quick results. The results will allow you to see their value quickly enough to build up belief in yourself and your goals. When you start seeing results that are helping you become the person you want to be, you will get addicted to change and be excited to implement new behaviors. The quicker you get addicted to growth, the better! Starting small and effective is what will keep you all-in when you start making more involved behavior changes that require bigger sacrifices. The key is consistency.

Let's put this into action! Grab your top 3 goals that you discovered in the last chapter, and list three long-term new behaviors that will get you to each goal. The healthy lifestyle example we used would look like this:

Goal 1 – Live a Healthy Lifestyle			
	New Behavior 1	New Behavior 2	New Behavior 3
Long-Term	Become a morning person	Eat 3 full healthy meals a day	Exercise 3 days a week
First Step	Get out of bed 15 minutes earlier	Eat breakfast (*doesn't have to be healthy yet*)	Park in the furthest spot away from every building I enter

Goal 1			
	New Behavior 1	New Behavior 2	New Behavior 3
Long-Term			
First Step			

Goal 2			
	New Behavior 1	New Behavior 2	New Behavior 3
Long-Term			
First Step			

Goal 3			
	New Behavior 1	New Behavior 2	New Behavior 3
Long-Term			
First Step			

CHAPTER 3

STEP 3: THE WHY

YOUR "WHY" IS your jet fuel for getting into action. It encompasses all the reasons for wanting to accomplish your goals. Your "Why" needs to be massive and irrevocable. Think about what hitting your goals will do for your life. Can you visualize what life will be like? Can you see the end before you get started? Your "Why" must be big enough and powerful enough that it will carry you through when times get tough. Trust me, there were plenty of tough times in my baseball career and there were plenty of times when I didn't feel like practicing, but my "Why" drove me to show up and be the best that I could be. My "Why" pushed me to stay in the zone and perform at my peak no matter my external circumstances. I pushed through the pain, showed up on the days I didn't feel like it, and did what needed to be done. Overcoming insurmountable obstacles became a regular part of my story because my "Why" was immovable.

In 1977, with the expansion of the Seattle Mariners becoming an MLB team, Dad was hired to be the pitching coordinator for the entire minor league system. It wasn't Yankee Stadium, but my older brother Mel Jr., my younger brother Jason, and I were back to roaming professional baseball fields. Minor league stadiums are the birthing grounds for future major league stars. I remember being on a trip with Dad where the rookie ball Mariners were playing against the rookie ball Padres in Walla Walla, Washington. The shortstop for the Padres was Ozzie Smith, who became a legendary hall of fame player. What I didn't know at the time was that I would be Ozzie's teammate with the St. Louis Cardinals two decades later. Life was great. Two years earlier Dad was our little league coach after ending his pitching career and now, with Dad back in baseball, we were hanging around the game all summer long on our favorite diamond-shaped playground.

After I spent a summer of fun with my brothers traveling with our dad from field to field, the winter of 1977 took a dramatic turn for the worse. My younger brother Jason got sick. His cold-like symptoms turned into days of lying on the couch with no energy. When the chest pains started, my parents decided it was time to return to the doctor. With blood work finished, my parents brought Jason home to rest. Before they could sit down at home, the phone rang and the doctor requested they return immediately for further testing. What we once thought was the common winter cold turned into a diagnosis of leukemia. Christmas was only weeks away, and my parents were taking Jason to Children's Orthopedic Hospital in Seattle, a couple of hours away from home, to meet with the cancer specialists and begin his first treatment. As a family, we were frightened. The word "Cancer" is a very scary word, especially when it lives in a seven-year-old boy.

That Christmas was very hard. We had just learned of Jason being diagnosed with leukemia and the last thing we wanted to do as a family was celebrate. It's very easy to assume the worst with cancer, but the doctors were assuring us that Jason had a good chance of survival and living a long life. The treatment would be very difficult for Jason because he would be medicated through his spine. He took the treatments and the chemotherapy like a champion, never once complaining about his treatments or his cancer.

Jason had a lust for life. I can still remember him running the neighborhood, butterfly net tightly grasped in his tiny seven-year-old hand flapping in the wind like a flag being carried into battle as he sprinted after every butterfly he saw. He loved birds, frogs, and all wildlife. He would study them through books, and he could identify them all, but he had a special love for butterflies. He would catch them and put them in jars until they died. He would read up on each one and then pin it to the ceiling above his bed. His room became an extension of the outdoors.

After months of treatment and losing his hair from the chemo, Jason went into remission and relief washed over our family. Maybe the doctors were right, and my little brother would beat this awful disease. We began to once again envision his future of studying insects and dominating every sport he played. Jason would wear hats to cover his baldness but, like everything else, he never complained. During his battle with cancer and fight to get into remission Jason continued demonstrating his love for sports by playing soccer, basketball, and baseball. He was an extraordinary athlete, and he excelled at all the sports he played. He was a natural on the baseball field, dominating every time he played. He played shortstop and was an unhittable pitcher in his little league games. No matter what sport he was playing, he was always the best player on the team.

Two years into remission, in 1980, despite our hopes and prayers that he would be cured, the leukemia returned. It was back to driving the two hours to The Seattle Children's Orthopedic Hospital where he would, once again, undergo treatments to fight the cancer. At only nine years old, the radiation and chemotherapy were hard on his body. My little brother was fighting for his life like the biggest champion I've ever witnessed. Jason never felt sorry for himself and never asked why he was going through what life was giving him. He confronted life's difficult times like a warrior, always thinking of the people around him and others with the disease. Every time we ate at a restaurant, Jason would fill in every slot where people could put in quarters for the fight against leukemia. He was focused on making a difference, not only for his fight but also for every child that was going through the same hell he was.

He went back into remission when he was 10 years old, but this time it only lasted a year and the leukemia returned for the third time. The doctors told us they could no longer control the disease with chemo and radiation. They advised my parents that Jason's best chance at living a long life would be a bone marrow transplant. Our whole family was tested to see who would be the best match to give the transplant. Every one of us would have done anything possible to help Jason. The doctors decided that I was the best match due to my blood and body type. It was my greatest honor. I prayed with all my might that my marrow would give Jason the life he deserved.

The procedure was grueling. I was put under at the hospital, and the doctors injected needles into my hips 260 times to draw the marrow out of my body and inject it into Jason through an IV. I remember waking up after the procedure in pain from head to toe. It hurt to move, but the pain only lasted about a day. The hope was that Jason's body would accept my marrow. The only concern the doctors had with the procedure was if Jason's body didn't accept the marrow, it would mean his death. At the time,

I'm not sure I understood the magnitude of the procedure, but I would have done anything to help save Jason.

The transplant was done, and it appeared to work. Jason seemed to be doing great. The doctors were very encouraged with Jason's progress. He was walking all over the hospital, and it seemed as if my little bro was back to being himself. Every day he was doing a little better to the point where we were all feeling like we would be going home soon. All of us were so excited that Jason was doing so well. The doctors told the family that Jason would be able to go home in a couple of days. They had a follow-up plan to see him every month to monitor his progress. Our hopes of traveling back to our home in Yakima as a family appeared to be a reality. However, about 10 days after the transplant Jason took a drastic turn for the worse. His body began to reject the marrow, and his organs began shutting down. The dream of Jason living a long life turned into a nightmare in a matter of days. His body went into a coma for about 48 hours and he died shortly after 2 a.m. on March 3rd, 1981, at only 11 years old.

We all were devastated. The transplant had appeared to work; we thought we would be going home together, and now my little brother lay in his hospital bed lifeless. My mom and dad stayed in the room with his body all night. I can't honestly remember where I was. I can only remember the guilt I felt. My marrow killed my little brother, and I knew it. Losing my little brother was hell but knowing my marrow killed him was double jeopardy. Initially, I did not draw on the conclusion that is was my marrow that killed him. We knew the marrow was his best and only shot at recovery. I was so upset and I remember wanting answers. Why did he look so good but then the coma and his death? My guilt was overwhelming. I understood the scope of the event and the opportunity to give him the greatest shot at life but it turned into a nightmare that ended his life. I hung on this and it felt like the demon in the details. I had no control over the situation, I didn't ever want anything to be left up to chance again. This became my life long battle.

That moment changed my life forever. Both my mom and dad tried to assure me that it wasn't my marrow that killed him. I love them so much for trying to protect me, but I was 15; I understood what had happened, and there was no changing how guilty I felt. It was the first time the whole world exploded into chaos around me and all I could see was what was right in front of me. It was the first time I encountered what "the zone" felt like, but it was the worst imaginable version of it.

Later that day we went home for the first time without Jason. The two-hour trip across the mountains seemed like an eternity. It is best described as my nightmare in slow motion. I don't recall any conversations. Even though we were all together, we were all caught up in our own sense of regret and thinking about our destination; Home without Jason. There was a silence that felt like a weight pressing on my chest that I could not remove. Opening the door into our house, my mom crumbled to her knees in violent sobs. It was absolutely the worst feeling in the world. Every limb in my body was numb while simultaneously in excruciating agony. The pain was too deep to fully feel but too real to be ignored. "If it weren't for my marrow we wouldn't be going through this," was the only thought grinding like a broken record in my mind. The echo of inconsolable sobs ringing through the house and reverberating through my own body was all that pulled me out of my daze. The house we now stood in, once so full of life, had lost its fullness and now felt empty. Every part of me was broken. Sad. Angry. I didn't know what to do next. Everything in me shut down. That's when dad stepped up and showed such wise leadership. Pulling us all together, we gathered in the living room as he told us that we would all stick together and never forget Jason. He would be with us forever.

As the days went on, I was having a tough time. I knew Jason was done suffering and had gone on to heaven, but I was living in hell without him. I was a sophomore in high school and I didn't want to go back to school. I wanted my lil' bro back and all I could think about was having Jason back. I am forever grateful to my father for leaving his baseball career after Jason died and staying home with Mel Jr. and me as we finished out our high school years.

Dad was home my last two years of high school, leaving his love of the game for his family. I needed him. I was living with so much pain from the loss of my little brother. It was always great having both my mom and my dad at every game I played in high school. You can't pick your parents, and I am grateful to have the greatest mom and dad in the world.

Jason's death changed my personality, I became this person who had to control everything, and when I couldn't, I'd snap. My dad writes in his book, *Pride and Pinstripes* that, "After Jason died…it was almost like Todd wanted to lash out at the world, take out his anger on everybody else. Sports gave him that sort of outlet. He played basketball and baseball with reckless abandon, and he was ready to challenge anybody at any time." Dad was right. The excruciating guilt lived inside of me. Ironically the need to be in control resulted in a loss of control as I played from the guilt and the anger that burned inside of me. Every time I competed, I played all out, with everything I had at that moment. Many times, my games would end in a fight if I didn't like the outcome. Something had snapped in me, and the result was a rage that made me a fierce competitor but it also threatened to derail my career.

What losing Jason did give me was an unshakeable "Why." In everything that I did, through every struggle and setback, Jason was my "Why." He left me with so many life lessons. I learned to take life one day at a time, never quit or give up, be courageous in the wake of the storm, never blame others, and think of others over myself the way Jason did. He truly taught me how to live. He was my reason for pushing past every career setback; he was why I fought with everything I had to reach my goal of playing in the MLB. Every time I wanted to complain about pain or exhaustion, my mind went to, "this is nothing in comparison to cancer." I remembered how when fighting cancer, Jason never complained and never stopped fighting, so I resolved to do the same. My goals held a new weight and urgency because I felt like they were no longer just mine, but ours. I wanted to honor his passion and dedication by putting my all into every dream I pursued. Whenever I'd think of Jason, the rest of the world would fade and I would find myself in "the zone" and laser-focused on whatever I needed to accomplish.

For me, the pain of staying the same would always come when I recognized my trajectory was threatening to make me fail. I didn't want to experience the feeling of failure I had when Jason's body rejected my marrow. I recognized that in life, some things are out of our control – no matter how much I wanted the bone marrow transplant to be successful, I couldn't control the outcome. So I committed to being in control of everything that I *did* have power over. I had a clear understanding of what was important in life, and what was worth being called a "challenge." So many of the challenges I faced in my career seemed minuscule in comparison to what I watched Jason fight, and that gave me the courage to keep pushing through the obstacles I faced. My "Why" is so personal and powerful, there is nothing that can take it away.

The key to having a "Why" that will drive you to succeed is to find something clear and unshakeable. It needs to be so powerful and meaningful to you that nothing anyone says or does can make you lose sight of your "Why." When you face setbacks, when you face negative opinions from others, you need to be rooted and grounded in your "Why," so you can push past the obstacles and continue fighting. If you are wondering how to identify your "Why," take some time to reflect on your *core identity*. What events or people have truly shaped who you are? What makes your success a "have to" instead of a "hope to"? Maybe your "Why" is the people your success will impact, rather than those who have already impacted you. If you have a clear vision of the lives that will be changed through your success, that too can become a firm and unshakeable "Why" that pushes you beyond what you thought was possible. *Clear* and *unshakeable* are the most important parts of your "Why."

Take some time to brainstorm possible sources of your "Why" from the categories mentioned.

My "Why" Brainstorm				
Category	People Who Have Shaped My Identity	Events That Have Shaped Me	Lives My Success Will Impact	Other
Brainstorm				
The "Why"				
Brainstorm				
The "Why"				
Brainstorm				
The "Why"				

Now that you've brainstormed through a few potential sources of your "Why," try to articulate it in 1 or 2 sentences. It's ok if you have more than 1 at this stage.

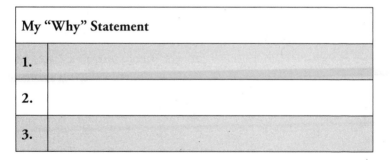

My "Why" Statement	
1.	
2.	
3.	

Narrowing down and being able to articulate your "Why" becomes the driving force behind everything you do; it gives you direction and purpose.

CHAPTER 4

STEP 4: BE WILLING TO SACRIFICE

WHAT SEPARATES THOSE who live world class from the rest of the crowd is the way they overcome obstacles and face their setbacks. In the face of adversity, the peak performers will be the people who have an unquenchable desire to reach their goals. Every goal worth pursuing will have setbacks, and that is when a willingness to sacrifice becomes essential in setting you apart to be a peak performer. With your goals, new behaviors, and unshakeable "Why" in your back pocket, you are ready to make the necessary sacrifices to start living world class.

In today's "I want it now" society we have become impatient and lost sight of what it means to sacrifice to achieve our goals. Successful people resist the shift towards instant gratification. They recognize that just because a goal takes time, dedication, and sacrifice doesn't mean it's impossible. What would you attempt to do if you were guaranteed to succeed? How big would you dream if you knew that you could hit every goal you ever set out to accomplish? How hard would you work if you knew it'd pay off? When you believe that everything is possible and within your reach you don't think, "What if I fail?" Making sacrifices is easy when you recognize that all sacrifice is short-term in comparison to the life you will live once your goals are accomplished.

The convenience we now experience in almost every aspect of life from fast-food to smartphones leads many to believe if something can't be accomplished quickly it won't be possible. This is why it is absolutely necessary to continue to hold onto your vision. Emmitt Smith says, "Vision gets the dreams started. Dreaming employs your God-given imagination to reinforce the vision. Both are part of something I believe is absolutely necessary to building the life of a champion, a winner, a person of high character who is consistently at the top of whatever game he or she is in."

Big vision mandates big sacrifice. Living world class is going to take time and consistent dedication. When you want a result bad enough the sacrifice becomes easy. You must place a higher value on the goal you're striving for than the things you must give up in the short-term. Achieving greatness is hard; if it were easy everyone would be living their dream life. There are going to be labor pains to birth your world class life. Jim Rohn once said, "We will all experience one pain or the other. The pain of discipline or the pain of regret, but the difference is that the pain of discipline weighs only ounces while the pain of regret weighs tons." Discipline is sacrificing where you are now to get where you want to go. Take a mental picture of hitting your goal. What does it look like? What does it feel like? What does it mean to you and your family or your company? If your goal or dream is big enough, the sacrifice will weigh far less than the regret of not pursuing it.

At 22-years-old, my lifelong dream of becoming a Major League Baseball player was right within my grasp. I had completed two seasons in the minor leagues with the Toronto Blue Jays and worked my way up to triple A. I was as close to the MLB as possible. However, my youth manifested in my inconsistency as a pitcher. After the grueling and physically taxing baseball season of continuous playing and traveling, many players use the winter offseason to rest, recover, or pick up a part-time job if you're a minor league player. My dad, brother, and I always set aside time for our annual hunting trip during the offseason. But the winter of 1987 was different, my sights were locked-in on finally making the MLB and fulfilling my childhood goal. I took one week off right when the season closed, and then I started training like never before. All I could think about was playing Major League Baseball. I hit the gym on a regular basis to gain as much strength as I could. The major league season is 162 games so I knew I needed to boost my overall strength and endurance. I turned every obstacle into a challenge, using every circumstance to enhance my training regimen.

Bundled from head to toe, I braced the snow and ice-covered roads for my nightly run. The sweat pouring from my face was unexpectedly soothing against the icy night air. With every step the ice threatened to put me on my face, just as my mind continually threatened to slip out of the zone. "You're gaining an edge," I would repeat to myself as I struggled to find motivation. "You're gaining an edge," I repeated, growing envious of my friend and trainer Bob Grimes who was following me in his warm truck, tracking my running speed. "It's freezing cold and I'm tired - NOPE - I'm gaining an edge." Running during those winter nights was a test of endurance and stabilization. Each step required increased body awareness and stabilization as I ran on the ice. Each minute required mental awareness and a stabilized vision of why I was pushing myself while everyone else was taking an offseason.

There may come a day in your pursuit of success when your sacrifice requires you to run on ice. Where every step requires intense concentration and care. When every necessary movement threatens to derail you, but stopping is not an option. You have to keep running; you have to pick up speed, and you have to trust that you can overcome the elements around you. You have to do what it takes to gain an edge. |

I began throwing on the very first day of 1988. I was focused on going into spring training in the best shape of my life. Training camp was six weeks away and my goal was to arrive at camp in mid-season form. I wanted to show the organization that I was ready, and that's exactly what I did. The Blue Jays had no intentions of me making the club out of spring training; they had me slated to start the season in triple A. I had an incredible spring. The Blue Jays kept pitching me and I kept mowing down major league hitters. The momentum was building and the press started to write that I looked ready for the MLB.

I was still around on the last day of spring training, but the team had to make one final cut. My heart sank when I was called into the manager Jimmy Williams' office after the final game. Walking to the chair across the desk from Jimmy, I knew I was settling in for a defining moment – this would either be the moment I've dreamt of for years, or the biggest career letdown of my life. I held my breath as he began to speak, "Congratulations Todd, you're going to be my fifth starter." A wave of relief and overwhelming excitement washed over me as I let out a deep exhale. I couldn't believe it. I was sitting at the very moment I'd dreamt of my entire life. I was officially a Major League Baseball player.

Every short-term sacrifice I had made in the offseason fully paid off in that moment. I had beaten the odds. I had gained an edge. I had trained to a level that no one expected from me to the point where my success was undeniable. I had earned my spot and proven myself throughout spring training. I was willing to sacrifice for where I wanted to go. I put in the time and did the work that many others were not yet willing to do. I reaped the immediate rewards that I was working towards in the offseason.

Accomplishing a goal doesn't mean the sacrifice is over. The harsh reality is when you push yourself to your peak performance you are just at the beginning of a higher level of success. You must never lose sight of what it took to gain success because once you get comfortable and think you have made it, you stand a greater risk of falling back. Staying at the top of your game and living *in* your goals takes just as much dedication, hard work, and sacrifice as getting *to* your goals.

Making the MLB in 1988 was just the beginning of many sacrifices to come. I quickly found out it was harder for me to stay in the big leagues than it was for me to get there. All my spring training success faded fast. Like the year prior I showed flashes of brilliance, but my overall inconsistency landed me back in the minor leagues by

August. My youth and inexperience couldn't maintain the high-level expectations placed on major leaguers. I spent the month of August in the minor leagues, and I dominated the hitters in Triple A. I knew I could do it, but I just had to prove it. I was called back up to Toronto in September to once again join the major league team. I saw limited action and on the last day of the season, I was told before the game that our general manager, Pat Gillick, wanted to see me before I left the stadium. I shuffled up to his office right after the game anxious to call it a year, go home, and enjoy some much-needed rest. I had worked relentlessly the past two seasons and pushed myself to train intensely through the previous winter break, so an offseason seemed much needed and well deserved.

"Todd, the organization wants you to go to winter ball and learn how to throw a new pitch," Pat said. I stared blankly at the wall behind him. I was frozen in disbelief and devastation. All the exhaustion from the prior year and half of nonstop grinding hit me like a freight train at that moment. I gritted my teeth as my whole body stiffened in anger. I felt defeated. It was as if all I had sacrificed was still not good enough. For a split second, I wondered if it was even worth the sacrifice of giving up another offseason in exchange for more intensive training. Sensing my discomfort at the situation Pat continued, "Todd, the only way you will make the club for the '89 season is if you go to winter ball and learn how to throw a slider."

My determination hooked onto three of Pat's words, "the only way." My momentary doubts were gone, and my decision was made—I was going to winter ball and I was going to make the club the following year. I was once again seeing the sacrifice in perspective. I knew the weight of the sacrifice was lighter than the pain of regret. It was a huge sacrifice; I moved to Venezuela for the two and a half months of winter ball where I pitched in their professional league to learn how to throw a slider. I had to live in a foreign culture where I didn't speak their language and they didn't speak mine. I missed Thanksgiving and Christmas with my family; I missed Mom's cooking. It was a huge sacrifice and I had to fight to keep the end goal of fulfilling my life-long dream in perspective. I went on to make the club in '89 and I'll elaborate on what happened from there in later chapters.

That winter wasn't the end of my setbacks or the end of my sacrifices; it was the beginning of saying "yes" to sacrifices. It marked the beginning of recognizing that sacrifices unlocked the opportunities to turn my goals into my realities. Something in Pat's words struck me. His words prompted me to wake up and take authority over the dreams and goals I had established for my life. "The only way" was exactly what I needed to hear. I needed to know that choosing to sacrifice was the only way to choose success.

No one said it was going to be easy. If you are aiming high, there are going to be many challenges along the way. You don't have to make major sacrifices forever. There will be times when you must adjust your life around your goal to do something significant and life changing. For me, it was putting my life on hold to spend 75 days in a foreign country playing baseball. The sacrifice was short compared to the 15 seasons living out my dream of playing in the MLB. You may have times in life where everything outside of your goal comes second for a short season. I promise you this, if your goals are big enough it will be worth it.

CHAPTER 5

STEP 5 – FIGHTING THE ENEMY

WHEN YOU ARE striving to live world class, enemies will come in all shapes and sizes. That is why step 5 of the Peak Performance method is "fighting the enemy." Now that you have said yes to making the necessary sacrifices to see your goals realized, you must be willing to engage in fighting your enemies. Making sacrifices involves pushing to achieve your goals while fighting your enemy requires learning what it takes to protect the vision you have established. When your goal is big, you will have plenty of small-thinking people who doubt your ability to achieve it. Growing up I was constantly bombarded with people asking what I was going to do if I didn't make it in the MLB since I "wasn't like my dad." I had to learn to let go of what other people thought or said about me. I knew in my heart that I was going to make it, even if my path to success didn't mirror my father's.

Not one person out there can keep you from your goals except for you. Don't give in; stay away from how the crowd thinks. Be the change that the crowd follows. Once you make it to your end goal, those same small-thinking people will be there saying "I knew you could do it!" as if they'd been supporting you all along. However frustrating this may be, you will become a role model and example for them to follow when they choose to turn away from their small-mindedness. But you were not born to live their small lives. You were meant to live world class!

Before we get into the specifics of how to fight your enemies, let's start with the necessary first step—identifying your enemies. Fighting your enemies is a proactive process. You must know who you're up against. You must know the strengths and weaknesses of the enemies you will encounter and what power they truly hold over you. Your enemy can be a lot of different things. It could be your current circumstances; the opinions of small-minded people that are spewing discouragement; health issues or physical injuries. Your enemy is anything standing in opposition to your goals. This can even be your own mindset. Your enemy can either destroy you or motivate you to push beyond what you previously thought possible.

My good friend Sam McDowell once told me, "What the mind can conceive and believe, it can achieve." You are going to become a person who brings the things you believe to life. If you believe other people's negative opinions, you are giving them a place to live in your life. However, if you choose to believe that you will succeed, you will bring to life this belief instead. Finding and fighting the enemy is about learning how to disempower the things that are opposing your success. Never accept the opinions of the people you wouldn't change places with.

My father, who was a five-time all-star pitcher for the Yankees, won 20 games, three separate times over the span of his 10-year major league career. The only time the Yankees reached the playoffs during his playing career was his first year in 1964. When I asked him how he won 20 games, three different times on teams that didn't even make it to the playoffs, he told me that every time he was the starting pitcher, he decided that the team was going to have a great day. He didn't listen to the sports radio shows that were saying how bad the Yankees were. He didn't buy into the enemy's opinions that threatened his success. He used the enemy as motivation. Against all odds, my dad took on the enemy and prevailed, and so can you.

My dad's enemy was a circumstance that he did not allow to overtake his commitment to greatness. The enemy can change from day to day and show up in places that you are not expecting. Sometimes it's obvious, like the opposing team during a competition, but usually, it's an internal battle with how you respond to the things threatening your success. My brothers and I faced the enemy of other people's opinions our whole lives.

Growing up with a famous father and wanting to follow in his footsteps made everyone feel like they had a right to be a commentator on my potential to achieve my dreams. This was not usually an encouraging process. Some of those people were close family friends. Some of those people were the parents of the kids that we were competing against. When we played well, the attitude from many of the parents was, "Well, of course they did well, they're the sons of an MLB legend!" But when we didn't do well, the tone shifted to, "What happened to them? They certainly aren't like their father!" It was as if our successes were not worth much, and our failures were scrutinized to no end. It's a blessing and a curse living in a world where everyone expects you to succeed. While it does open a few opportunities that not everyone has access to, there is immense pressure to live up to the expectations everyone has formed for you. Additionally, when those expectations are based on someone else's achievements, rather than your own, it can feel like an impossible enemy to face.

I had to learn early, how to not take on those expectations, and how to not give life to other people's negative opinions. If you don't allow the opinions of the enemy any room in your life, then they will remain *false* opinions and are carried away by the wind they were spoken into. Fortunately, the pressure to replicate our father's career was not perpetuated by our parents. My dad used to tell us all the time, "Whatever you guys do, just be the best at it that *you* can possibly be." It was our choice to follow in his footsteps and pursue professional baseball.

Our parents had instilled in us a winning mindset towards whatever we chose to do with our lives. When I made it to the major leagues, the comparisons to my father circled back. I had finally made it to where I had always dreamed of being and now I was living under the umbrella of "He's not like his father." The media loved to make that noise, but a lifetime of hearing it had taught me to stay focused on just being the best that *I* could be, never competing with my father's career. I never had a backup plan in case baseball didn't work out. I wasn't thinking about it not working out. I was completely sold on playing in the major leagues.

From the time I could walk, I saw myself playing in the big leagues. To hit your goals, especially if they are big goals, there is no room for thinking, "What if I don't make it?" That kind of attitude makes you your own worst enemy. You will have plenty of enemies to fight without adding yourself to the count! You need to be your biggest cheerleader because there will be times where everything and everybody are telling you success isn't possible. In those moments, you need to know your value and ability, and you need to believe that you can and will succeed!

The most prominent memory I have of using the enemy's opinion as motivation happened in 1991. I was playing for the Toronto Blue Jays and we were up against the Texas Rangers in Arlington. Nolan Ryan was on the mound for the Rangers. I sat and watched as 44-year-old Ryan mowed down one Blue Jay hitter after another—the 7th no-hitter of his career. I'll admit I was inspired by how he didn't let the "enemy" of his age stand in the way of dominating the hitters who were half his age. Five days later we were playing the Rangers again, this time in Toronto. Nolan Ryan was once again the starting pitcher for the Rangers, but this time I would not be watching the game from the dugout because I was the starting pitcher for the Blue Jays.

Every sports network was talking about the miraculous Nolan Ryan who had just thrown his 7th no-hitter at the age of 44. Nolan was a living legend, and he deserved all the media attention that he was getting. He was a true professional and certainly one of the best of all time. I was a big fan of Nolan's, but on game day, he was the enemy. I had a job to do, and that was to be my best that night pitching against this powerhouse. I sat in my chair in front of my locker in the Blue Jays' clubhouse prior to the game, watching The Sports Network (TSN), mentally preparing myself to take on Nolan Ryan and the Rangers. Lacing up my spikes, all I heard from the TV was the buzz about how Nolan might make history that night by throwing the first back-to-back no-hitter. Glancing up at the screen I was bombarded with the highlight reels from five days earlier when Nolan was mowing down my team's hitters. My motivation grew with every clip and comment, and I stood up to head out to the bullpen.

Right on cue, as if the universe knew I needed an extra push, our hometown sportscaster said flippantly, "And if anyone cares, Todd Stottlemyre is the starting pitcher for the Toronto Blue Jays tonight." Now fuming, I glared at the screen and snapped back.

"I'll show you!" I clicked it off and headed to the field ready to fight for this win with everything in me. I pitched seven and two-thirds innings, held the Rangers to two runs, and we won four to two. My enemy that night showed up on a television right before I headed to warm up. He gave me the little extra push in my mindset to rival one of the best pitchers in the history of the game of baseball. My choice to fight this commentary rather than believe it gave us the edge to win. I chose to believe in my ability and my goal, beyond the opinions of others or the external circumstances, clearly laid out before me as this legendary pitcher had just demolished my team five days prior.

I'm not claiming that believing in yourself will make

choose ①.

success a smooth-sailing process. What I'm saying is this; in your pursuit of success you will face intense setbacks, you will be up against enemies that seem impossible to defeat, and you will have to face challenges where the odds are insurmountably stacked against you. You may even be bombarded with a number of setbacks all at once where you feel so buried in trials and surrounded by enemies that you have no idea how you will make it to the end of the day, much less to your end goal. When those times come - because they will - you need to be in a place where you are willing to stare down the enemy and fight through whatever cards life hands you. You need to know that your dreams are worth fighting for, that you are valuable enough to sacrifice for so that you can see the rewards on the other side. You need to know that you can and will succeed, and giving in to the enemy or becoming your own enemy will not get you through the setbacks.

In 1999, I entered spring training after signing a 4-year contract with the Arizona Diamondbacks. I was excited about the future. Jerry Colangelo owned the club, and he assured me that he was building a team that could win a World Championship during my 4 years. I was in the prime of my career, and I had high hopes of being an integral part of helping the team live out the vision of a World Championship victory. Colangelo pulled together a great team. He had signed Randy Johnson, Greg Swindell, Steve Finley, Luis Gonzales, and others to join the existing team led by veterans Matt Williams and Jay Bell. The future looked bright for the Arizona Diamondbacks and in early spring the media had slotted us to be a strong contender for the World Championship. Occasionally after training, I'd make the 2-hour drive from my spring training apartment in Tucson to check on things at my new house in Phoenix.

One rainy day, that drive forever changed my life. I answered a call from my father, who was in spring training as the pitching coach with the New York Yankees. After the first few minutes of small talk there were a few long seconds of silence before dad continued, "Son, I have something I need to tell you." I could tell by the shift in his tone, something was off. "I was given a second blood test after my physical screening because my first was a little bit unusual. The second test confirmed that the proteins in my blood cells are off, and I was diagnosed with a blood cancer called Multiple Myeloma." I continued driving, shocked and speechless, although I don't even remember the drive. Hearing the word "cancer" again for the first time since losing Jason sent piercing agony through my body. Involuntary tears broke through my best attempts to hold myself together. Dad continued, "They found it early enough that it's actually too early to treat. Don't worry, I'm going to beat this thing." I didn't know what to say or how to respond. I wanted to believe he would beat it, but the harsh reality of cancer hit too close to home with all of us. I don't remember how the call ended, but I pulled off the freeway because I could no longer see through my tears. As the rain poured down outside, I felt as if the world was sharing my pain and attempting to drown me at the same time.

I called my mom later that night and she assured me that dad was going to be ok, echoing that the cancer was found early and it was too early to treat. My parents are the strongest people I have ever met. They battle circumstances like warriors, with not one ounce of quit in them, and they never lose focus on their vision. Our family and the Yankees were the only ones who knew of Dad's cancer, and that's the way my parents wanted it. Dad stayed focused on his job, being the best coach he could possibly be for his Yankee pitchers.

I got off to a great start with the Diamondbacks going 4-1 into my start against the San Francisco Giants on May 17th. I woke up that morning with a stiff shoulder but didn't give it much thought. I had been mostly healthy my whole career, so I didn't think much of a little shoulder ache even knowing I was pitching that night. Warming up in the bullpen before the game our pitching coach Mark Conner asked if I was all right. I told him I was fine apart from a little ache in my shoulder that I was having a tough time getting loose. Finishing up in the bullpen, the game began and all my thoughts were on getting the Giants' hitters out. After the first inning, my shoulder started to get worse. It felt much like a toothache in my shoulder. As each inning progressed, it got worse. Our offense was on fire and we had a big lead as I took the mound in the fifth. My first warm-up pitch didn't even reach the plate. Our manager Buck Showalter and our pitching coach Mark Connors came running out of the dugout to the mound.

"Todd, what is going on?" Buck asked. "Are you hurting?"

"I have a bit of a shoulder ache," I replied, "but I want to throw one more pitch and see if I can stay in the game."

Once again, the pitch didn't even reach the plate and I was in intense pain.

"Nope, that's it, Todd," Buck said.

"But I want to keep trying!" I pushed back.

"No. You're done for the night," he said, turning to walk back to the dugout.

I headed for the showers extremely frustrated. I had a big lead and I wanted the win, but mostly I was frustrated that my shoulder was killing me and I didn't know why.

The next morning I flew back to Arizona to meet with Dr. David Zeman, our team's head doctor and orthopedic surgeon. After examining my shoulder, he sent me to get an MRI. The first MRI was inconclusive and the second

MRI revealed a hole in my rotator cuff and a tear in my labrum and bicep tendon. My arm was in severe disrepair. Dr. Zeman encouraged me to get other opinions, saying that with the severity, he could fix my shoulder surgically but it would likely be a career-ending decision. I was devastated. I set up an appointment with the famous Los Angeles-based orthopedic surgeon, Dr. Lewis Yocum.

Dr. Yocum took one look at my MRIs and then looked at me and said, "Well, you've had a good career. Your shoulder can be fixed surgically, but you will probably never pitch in Major League Baseball again." I was crushed; career-ending circumstances came out of nowhere. I was off to a great start with the Diamondbacks and feeling good with the exception of the May 17th game. Upon returning to Arizona, I met with Dr. Zeman to reassess my options. I was not willing to surrender to this career-ending enemy without a fight.

Dr. Zeman offered to build a program where I could gain as much strength in my body as possible, especially around my shoulder, and alter my pitching mechanics to use my body more effectively to protect my injured shoulder. The other option was doing the surgery and hoping for the best. Either way, no one thought I would pitch again that year, except for me. I took one look at Dr. Zeman and said, "Build the strength program. I'm not only going to pitch again, I'm going to be back this year." I walked out of his office and right into the weight room to begin the strength-training process. At that moment, I was totally focused on my vision of pitching again in the major leagues. The easy road would have been to call it a career and sit back and collect a check for the next 4 years. No way was I giving in to these career-ending circumstances. The opportunity to beat all the odds consumed my every thought.

I woke up every day with the vision of making it back to the big leagues. I was on a mission. I spent every day in the weight room. There was no time for days off. Three grueling months later, on August 20th, I shocked the baseball world by being the starting pitcher for the Arizona Diamondbacks against the Pittsburg Pirates. I pitched four and two-thirds of an inning. I might have lost the game, but I had won the war against my enemy.

Dr. Zeman wrote me the following letter just prior to my return on the 20th:

Dear Todd:

I wanted to write you a note to let you know just how very proud I am of you and what you have accomplished. You have shown such tremendous courage and character in your journey to recovery. Very few people truly understand the severity of your shoulder injury and have yet to realize the true significance of your miraculous recovery. It is nothing short of legendary. You are a legend in all sense of the word. You are unbelievably special to have overcome these obstacles with such ease, it is obvious to me that you had to draw from your inner strength. I imagine that you have reached an area of your mind and soul that few people ever experience. It truly is a gift from God to know how to reach the heights that you have climbed.

After you win the World Series this year and then pitch for another three to five years, you can probably relax, but you will always have the ability to reach that inner strength to meet the challenges that we all face in life. But for now just remember, you have the stuff that legends are made of. You have overcome obstacles that few, if any, have ever done before. You have reached a height that no one else has dared to climb.

You may not be aware of this, but you must be such a tremendous inspiration to your teammates. I'm sure that they have all recognized your tremendous courage and character. I think you exemplify what this team has been all about this year. This is a very special year and in my eyes, you are the most special thing about it. I am very proud of you and I have tremendous respect for you and your abilities. I am quietly a very prayerful person and I will be praying for you constantly all of Friday until you have thrown your last pitch.

May Godspeed and strength be with you. I only wish I could be there to witness your success. I truly hope that you experience unbelievable joy on Friday. You certainly deserve it. Have great fun and great luck!

Sincerely,
David Zeman, M.D.

Needless to say, this letter has a special place in my heart. Receiving this letter from Dr. Zeman was worth every ounce of the grind to making it back and staying focused on my vision. We didn't win the World Series in 1999, but I took great pride in pitching game two of the playoffs against the Mets and helping the Diamondbacks secure their first playoff win in franchise history. I pitched six and two-thirds innings and walked off to a standing ovation in front of a sold-out stadium in Arizona.

That winter I continued to work out in the weight room like an animal. I couldn't afford to lose any strength. Dad was getting routine blood tests to monitor his cancer and all seemed to be well. I went into spring training stronger than ever. I was ready to take on the grind of a long season with a torn-up shoulder. Spring training went great and it was time to start the season. I won my first start against the Phillies but the game left a burning sensation in my elbow. Our trainer, Dr. Sheridan, told me I had a subluxation of the ulnar nerve which means my nerve was floating around outside the groove. Dr. Sheridan immediately said I needed surgery to put the ulnar nerve back into its groove. Surgery on my elbow not only meant being out but also losing all the strength I had built up to protect my shoulder. I told them I would pitch as long as I could before having surgery on my elbow.

A few days later as I pulled my car into the stadium, my dad called. After the usual catching up, he went on to say that his most recent blood test revealed the cancer was big enough to start treating. He reiterated that he had a great doctor and that he was going to beat this awful disease. He reminded me that I had to take good care of myself and not worry about him. However, the doctors predicted he had about 3-years to live, even with treatment. Receiving the call was brutal; it was like hearing about his cancer for the first time. Dad was having a press conference later that day. Up until now, his Yankees co-workers and our family were the only ones who knew of my father's condition.

Dad explained how he might have to miss some games due to his treatment and that it was unfair to his pitchers and all the fans to keep it a secret any longer. As we hung up, I sat in my car fighting the tears and emotions. The Diamondbacks PR director Mike Swanson met me as I walked through the clubhouse doors. He was alerted by the Yankees of the press conference with my father. Mike knew that I would have to face our local media and answer questions as soon as the news of my father got out. I was mentally preparing myself to stand tall in light of the grueling circumstances. The condition of my arm seemed like such a small ordeal compared to what my father was going through back in New York. I was back to training and fighting the enemy of my pain based on my "Why" of "this is nothing in comparison to cancer."

A couple of weeks later we traveled to Philadelphia to play the Phillies, and I was pitching. The Yankees had a day off the night of our game. My mom called and said she and dad were driving to Philadelphia to watch me pitch. For the first time in my 10-year MLB career, my father would be in the stands watching my game. I was extremely excited to be leaving tickets in my father's name for the first time. Our traveling secretary, who took care of the players' tickets, came to ask if my dad being on the pass list was a joke since it was unusual for the Yankees to have an off day. I asserted that they were indeed coming to the game. They sat my parents in the front row right next to our dugout.

Since this was a national league game, I would be hitting for myself rather than employing the designated hitter that pitchers use in the American league. I was nervous since batting is not my expertise and my parents were in the audience. I put my nerves and pain into perspective—I'm fighting to win a game while my hero sits in the stands, fighting for his life. As adrenaline pumped through my veins, chemo pumped through his. This game was for him. Stepping up to the plate, fully in the zone forgetting about my own pain, I swung at the first pitch with all my might. I heard the connecting clang and ran for first, realizing quickly the ball had cleared the fence over left center field. I hit it out of the park. I hit my first and only homerun of my entire MLB career and my parents were there to see it. The momentum continued and I went on to be the winning pitcher for the game, as the Diamondbacks defeated the Phillies.

My parents were escorted into the tunnel just outside the clubhouse doors so we could talk briefly before they headed back to New York. Dad took one look at me and said, "Todd, how are you doing it?" My blank stare led him to continue, "How in the world are you pitching through all the pain you're in and still winning with a torn-up shoulder and elbow?" He was referring to my torn labrum, the hole in my rotator cuff and the fact that my ulnar nerve had subluxated and basically had come out of its groove inside my arm.

I looked back at my father, knowing his chemo pump was still on under his jacket and said, "No, Dad how are *you* doing it?"

Knowing that my father was undergoing chemo treatment as he continued to pursue his coaching career with the Yankees, confirmed to me his focus on "there is life after cancer." But my pain just didn't compare to what dad was going through. This wasn't something that was going to kill me. Dad didn't realize that he was my inspiration to continue to fight, continue to do what it took even with the intense pain. My pain just didn't feel like that big of a deal compared to what he was going through.

He replied with his go-to saying during this battle, "Living life to the fullest, with cancer."

My father never complained or gave power to the enemy of his circumstances. He refused to let cancer slow him down. He stayed focused on his vision, his passions, and his goals. My perspective was simple: if my Dad could keep his passion for the game while he was fighting for his life, how could I not keep going just because I had pain in my arm? I was only fighting for one more game each time I stepped on the field and he was fighting for his life. My enemy was comparatively minuscule; I had to overcome it. My dad had always inspired me from the time I roamed the grounds of Yankee Stadium, but now he was taking it to a whole new level. He is the ultimate champion.

For both of us, our enemy became our health issues. My father continued to work as the pitching coach with the New York Yankees while he was fighting even with the estimated 3 years left to live. He found a way to keep going no matter what the enemy was telling him about his health. This gave me the inspiration to continue competing against the enemy of my torn shoulder and elbow. If my dad could continue pursuing his dreams and dedicate his time and energy to his team in the face of a life-threatening disease, I would continue to fight against my career-threatening injuries. It became a game to see how far I could go.

It's been over 16 years since my father's diagnosis (and the estimated 3 years left) and his determination and passion has taken down every enemy he's encountered. He continues to fight, and he will forever continue to inspire. Just as Lance Armstrong writes in his book about how his cancer diagnosis pushed him to his first Tour de France victory, it's not about the dedication to the sport but the journey back to life.

That's what facing your enemies is; a journey back to life. But beyond that, it's a battle and a journey into living world class. When you are facing your enemies, fighting with everything in you and conquering them, you are performing at your peak. It's impossible to be a peak performer without your enemies—there is value in the fight. But you must keep the enemies in the right position. You must maintain power over the things that threaten to derail you, and you must continue to be committed to conquering your enemies. When you feel hopeless or you feel like giving up, you need to look for your enemies. You need to identify what is threatening to hold you back and you need to fight like hell to overcome them. Look at your goals, change your behaviors, hold onto your "Why," make the sacrifices that need to be made, and remind yourself and your enemy that *you* determine your success, not the enemies that are waging war against you.

Your fight must be **relentless** because your enemies will be. If you back down, the enemy will win. So many people give up just one step away from victory. You will not be one of those people if you cling to the Peak Performance method with relentless devotion. There are no rewards for playing small. Like my father said, "Whatever you do be the best at it that *you* can be." Your relentless devotion and fight will not look like anyone else's. To be the best, you have to outwork the rest. Talent or circumstance may get you in the race, but you won't win without hard work. Once you have identified and begun to fight your enemies, you must fully commit to your decision to succeed.

Identifying and defeating specific enemies is a huge victory in moving forward with your goals. You will learn that it is possible to turn bitter circumstances and doubting peers into even greater strengths. But sometimes the enemy isn't a concrete outside force; sometimes the temptation to quit can come from within; self-doubt, lack of belief, the self-sabotaging behavior we can allow when we are just steps from victory; when it seems like our dreams turn against us. In the next chapter, we will discuss how to move forward even when fighting doesn't fix the problem.

CHAPTER 6
STEP 6 – DECISION TIME

NOW THAT WE are over half-way through the Peak Performance method, it's time to address the most difficult topic—what do you do if you've been doing all the right things, but you aren't seeing the success you expected? What happens if you feel like you've done everything in your power to be the best you can be and to fight for your success? You've followed all the steps to a T and maybe even reached a level of success that was greater than what you've ever experienced, but circumstances led you to losing it all. Then what? As I mentioned in the last chapter, there were times in my MLB career where I came close to losing it all due to external circumstances. From making the majors and being repeatedly pushed back to the minors, to injuries that should have been career-ending, I used my method to push through the challenges, face my enemies, and overcome opposition with hard work and dedication.

All major successes come through lots of little failures along the way. When the road gets bumpy or you are thrown off the road entirely and aren't sure if you will make it out with your dreams intact, that is when you have reached the critical point I call "Decision Time." Every major goal that I have pursued has had a clear decision time where I've stepped back, re-evaluated why I was pursuing whatever was in front of me, and decided which goals and dreams were worth pursuing wholeheartedly at that time. I had to ask, "Which goals am I still burning to accomplish? What am I still willing to sacrifice everything for? What is still worth a whole-hearted fight?"

This is a critical turning point where you will either decide to fight harder than ever before or re-adjust your plan and walk away from your previous dreams and goals in pursuit of others. Typically, this is a dark, tumultuous season where you are forced to reflect on what circumstances, good or bad, got you to where you are now, realistically evaluate your current situation, hold firm to your vision and goal for the future, and decide what is next for you. My advice is this; if your dreams and goals are still burning inside of you, do not let them go, no matter how impossible it may seem at that moment. Make the decision to continue to fight to see your goals accomplished. You've already done the hard work of committing to your goals, changing your behaviors, sacrificing, and removing the enemies' influences. You are incredibly close to your breakthrough, and now would be the absolute *worst* time to walk away. However, if you are a passionate person who has many goals and a broad vision, this is the time to refine that. Discover what still lights the fire in you and puts you in the mentality of a peak performer, and fully commit to those goals.

My first day in retirement from the MLB felt like any other first day off after a long season. It was a welcomed respite and an opportunity to spend time with family, plan family vacations around the kids' winter break, and go on some hunting and fishing trips with my father and my brother. I was proud that I had given my baseball career everything I had mentally, emotionally, and physically. I knew that I had left every pitch that I had in my right arm on the field. I felt at peace about my health-related forced retirement because there was nothing left for me to give. I had no regrets or wonders about whether I could still play at the major league level; I was ready to take on other aspects of my life and explore other passions. My goal was to take one year off to spend quality time with my wife and our five amazing kids before I committed to a new career. I had made millions of dollars living out my dream and we were financially set for life. I had plenty of time to think about the next phase. I spent lots of my down time planning our family vacations for the year.

Spring training was approaching fast and it was my first

spring not going to camp. All my buddies were coming to town with the excitement of another season in Major League Baseball, and for the first time since retiring, I felt left out. I was not prepared for the feeling of being lost. I missed the camaraderie of the guys getting back together. I was an outsider for the first time and it was tough being away from the diamond. I had turned down lots of different jobs to stay committed to a year off with my family, so we booked a trip to Hawaii to escape the familiar routine of spring training.

One year off sounded good in theory, but I hated retirement. I needed to be working at something. I had lost my identity as a professional athlete and I was ready to take on the next part of my life. I just didn't have a clear vision of what that looked like. I loved business and the financial markets, and my neighbor and good friend, Alan Fonner, was the director of the local area for a Wall Street firm.

Over a dinner that my wife, Erica, set up, Alan offered me an opportunity. He felt I would be a perfect fit for the competitive environment. Since I loved the stock market, I went to Alan's office the following week to discuss the opportunity and I left the meeting with a job. I was no longer in retirement; I had a job that gave me a new purpose and a new field to dominate. After passing the Series 7 exam on financial markets and regulations, I had to pass a state test on Blue Sky Laws. The security markets are a heavily regulated industry and everyone who participates must go through the labor-intensive exams. I was also being trained by the local office manager, Dave Dorward. Dave was not just a manager; he also had a big book of clients whose investments he was overseeing through the firm. Four months in, with no prior experience, I was fully licensed with the Series 7, state test, insurance license, and even my commodities license.

I knew I was being heavily recruited because of my competitive background and all the millionaires I had in my contact list, but I didn't want to join someone else's team. I wanted to build my own team. Since Dave Dorward was the guy who trained me, and I liked his integrity, he was the first person I approached about teaming up. He was all in and brought two of his teammates on board with us to form the Stottlemyre Group. Each guy brought their own expertise and resources to the group, and everyone's differences worked together seamlessly to create a first-class advisory team. I was proud of what I had assembled in a short period. Eight months earlier I was a major league pitcher and now I was leading a seasoned investment team at a high-powered Wall Street firm.

It was game time, and the first step was to go out and start building a client base. I started with family and close friends and worked with the same fervor I had playing baseball. People could feel my commitment and passion, and that earned their trust. I was selling the expertise of the team that I had put together and the firm behind us. Just like in baseball, I knew I would win some and lose some. I stayed committed to the process of going through the numbers and didn't worry about it when people chose not to do business with me. I closed a 5-10 million dollar account my first week.

Soon after my first week, I attracted a public company as a client and they put 20 million into a cash account and moved over their 401k business. I was focused and brought the same discipline to the firm that I had in Major League Baseball; first one to the office and last one to leave. I was on a mission to win big. I learned very quickly that succeeding in business is much like sports. I had to learn from every failure but at the same time move on very quickly, focusing on learning new skills that would create success. I had to develop new behaviors that would become habits, stay committed to the process, and have the desire to persist when the going got tough.

We had created a massively successful team in just a few short years, managing hundreds of millions of dollars. Just before my five-year anniversary at the firm, I woke up not wanting to go to the office. I was tired of working for someone else and I wanted to create my own company. I loved my team and the business, but I wanted out and to run an investment fund. I went into the director's office to let him know I would be leaving the firm. I assured him I was not going to another firm and stayed an extra 30 days to meet with all our clients, letting them know they were in good hands with the team that I built. In short, I was doing everything I could to help the firm retain the clients, and left on good terms. I owed it to both the firm and the clients to let them know my plans because these people trusted me and I wanted to honor their trust.

I took a short break before diving into creating my own investment fund, accumulating and starting businesses with friends and colleagues along the way. I was the largest shareholder of a golf course management company in Florida where we owned a few courses and ran a couple of others. I owned one-third of a student loan company, had investments in a few technology companies, and bought real estate as rental properties. I even threw some money into a few social media companies. I was collecting companies and assets on my way to building an empire.

I was very active in the stock market, owning large positions in some big names like Apple and writing calls on positions I owned and creating cash flow. After I left the firm, I was trading daily, making large bets one position at a time, and I was crushing the stock market. I don't want to claim to be an expert because the market was in a bull market and everyone was winning. Companies like Google, Apple, and Goldman Sachs were exploding and I owned them all. Everything we owned was doing great; we were printing money. There were months where I was making more money than when I played major league baseball.

As an example of just how large we were living in this season, we took a two-week family vacation to Hawaii, spending one week in Maui and one week in Kona. We downgraded from our usual private jet to the whole family flying first class on a major airline. Between the first class tickets, multiple rooms at 5-star resorts, and countless incredible meals, our two-week vacation added up to about $40,000. We were living in the lap of luxury and not sparing a penny. This lifestyle was all being funded by my businesses and the stock market. During that two-week trip I was getting up at 3 a.m. and trading the market and then at breakfast on the beach with the family by market close, which was 10 a.m. Hawaii time. I was killing the market and having an incredible world class vacation with my family at the same time. In those two weeks, I made over $400,000 in the stock market, so we didn't even feel the $40,000 expense for the trip.

Not every business venture was a massive success, but we could overcome the losses because when we were winning, we were winning *big*. If we lost on a business, we figured out where we went wrong and started over because there was money to be made. The money for me was nothing more than a scoreboard. I was playing a game.

My wife would ask, "How much is going to be enough?" but the draw for me wasn't about having enough, it was about seeing how much I could score and moving my goals higher and higher. I remember telling Erica that I was going to be a billionaire. I was addicted to the game of matching businesses with the right team and I started to feel invincible. I was on the daily prowl for the next opportunity. There was always a business to start or a business to buy into, properties to turn into rental income, trades to be made in the stock market. I was pitching a game every day and our empire was growing.

Life was great, everyone in my family was healthy, and I had found a new passion: building businesses and multiplying my assets. We were living the American dream in our beautiful 8,000-square-foot home in Paradise Valley, Arizona. Our home had doubled in value in a few years; we had nice cars and traded them in every couple of years and purchased new ones in cash. Our five kids, Rachael, Madison, Ava, Todd Jr., and Brooklyn were all enrolled in private school. We took private jets for all domestic vacations, and I even flew private when I went on fishing and hunting trips. There was nothing quite like pulling my Mercedes into the private airport in Scottsdale, climbing directly onto the plane, letting the pilot know I was ready, and being airborne minutes later.

Arriving back in Scottsdale after my trip, the airport

staff pulled my freshly detailed car straight up to the plane. I was home within minutes. It was my greatest luxury. There was a big price tag on flying private but it was never a thought because big money was coming in fast. We became easy targets for all the local charities because we were known for never turning down anyone or any cause. When my wife and I attended fundraising events, they could count on us to donate thousands of dollars or, in some cases, tens of thousands of dollars.

My businesses were growing and I was adding new companies and investments to my portfolio constantly. I started using leverage from my cash flow and assets to buy new opportunities. I thought about paying my house off, but I just couldn't make sense of it. I was getting the tax write off, it had doubled in value, and I wanted to invest every possible dollar to increase my financial scoreboard. Because of the spike in my home's value, I used it as a cash machine to fund new opportunities. It was a crazy time. The money was coming in so fast that it was almost too easy. I remember telling Erica there's no way this could continue; everyone was making money in the stock market, and everyone was making a killing in the real estate markets, and I was no different. My logical side told me to get out, or at least start paring back and protecting my assets, but my fear of getting out early and missing out on big money was too great. Fear and greed kept me in the game when I knew in my gut I should scale back. When amateurs are making a killing, you know it's time to head for the sidelines, but as an avid competitor, I didn't want to sit out of the game. I was playing to win and leveraging all my assets to the hilt, praying the bull market would continue and I wouldn't be left out when the music stopped.

The Dow Jones Industrial Average peaked on October 9th, 2007, and a couple of days later hit an intra-day high of 14,198.10. It's impossible to know when the high hits in the market until long after it's over. Many of the top professionals were calling for a 10-20% decline which would be a normal pullback after a bull market. By mid-March of 2008, the market had in fact declined by 20%. All my companies and security accounts could handle a recession and a 20% decline. But I was most concerned about the leverage that I had used to add assets to my portfolio.

As the security accounts were dropping, the pressure was mounting. I was too greedy and competitive to get out, but being all-in was terrifying. Some professionals were predicting a collapse, while others were saying we might be at the bottom and could be on the upswing shortly. I was afraid if I got out now I would miss the possible rebound and the chance to recover my losses. Markets continued to tumble, the banking system was under pressure, and people in this great country had lost faith in our banks. My portfolio was dropping, which put massive pressure on me and the leverage that I had against those security accounts. Once again, investment professionals were calling for the bottom to be in the market with the fall of both Lehman Brothers and the takeover of Merrill Lynch by Bank of America.

In hindsight, that would have been a great time to get out if you were still in the market, but who knew what was yet to come? I was scared to get out of the market at the bottom, but I was also afraid to stay in the market because of all the pressure that was mounting on my loans. I knew that this could not go on forever and sooner or later the nightmare of this downturn would be over. It wasn't over. It was only about the 4th or 5th inning, but the scoreboard didn't have an end to it and no one knew when the game would be over. It wasn't just the loss in value on my stock portfolio that was killing me; I had borrowed money against the portfolio when the market was thousands of points higher to buy real estate that was set up to produce a rental income.

I felt lucky to sell my golf course and golf course management company before the heat of the downturn to a group of pastors in Florida who wanted to turn the sport and its property into a ministry. I took back a second mortgage of one million dollars to personally help them buy me out. I thought two things: firstly, the money was safe and they would pay me interest, and secondly, I was selling to a group that wanted to do something great with the business. The problem was that because of the downturn people stopped playing golf and the group who I sold to walked from the course, leaving the bank and me empty handed. Losing one million dollars this way made me bitter because I felt like I got screwed over for doing a good deed.

I lost another million dollars overnight when the federal government shut down the student loan business I had built. I had invested into a technology company that was now going under due to a lack of liquidity, so I said goodbye to another five hundred thousand dollars overnight. Many other private companies that I had invested in were starving for capital. I was getting hit from every angle; my financial empire that was funded by 15 seasons of Major League Baseball was under siege by a fallen and broken economy.

I was hanging on by the seat of my pants, praying that the bottom was in the market after Bear Stearns, Lehman Brothers, Merrill Lynch, and many other companies fell and we lost nearly 4,000 points off the top in the stock market. Once again, many market professionals were calling for the bottom to be in place but what scared the hell out of me was that others were calling for more to come. I didn't know who was going to be right, but I was still invested and riding the worst roller coaster of my life. I kept thinking, "I just need to get through this year and then everything will be all right." I could make back the money lost eventually. In hindsight, it's so easy to see that I should've gotten out sooner. The fight of whether to stay in or get out was an emotional nightmare. I was at my lowest low and wasn't sure if I would ever get out or if I could wait until a rescue team arrived with a ladder that would allow me to climb back out.

We were in the middle of a global meltdown and the worst was still yet to come. I was sleeping very little and my stress was at an all-time high. The only thing worse than never having money is having it and losing it, and I was on the verge of losing it all. After the record drop on September 29th, 2008, my accounts had lost between thirty and forty percent. My home that was valued close to $4 million at the height had lost about $2 million in value. I was still invested and hanging on. At this point, I felt like I had no option but to ride this out. The bottom was coming; it just couldn't get here fast enough. Every day I would get up and lock myself in my home office in total solitude to make decisions on our future. I was completely removed from my family. I was doing everything I could to hang on. I would calculate the losses in our portfolio at the end of every day. From my office chair, I would then throw the calculator against the back of my wooden office doors. My wife would know by the sound of the exploding calculator that it was another bad day in the markets.

To put the situation in perspective, there was one day where I was in a good mood for the first day in months.

Erica asked, "You look happy, did we make money today?" I replied, "No, but we only lost $150 thousand today!" Can you imagine when losing 150K signals the best day you've had in months? 2008 came to an end and I was hoping that 2009 would bring better times. The market continued its downward slope in 2009 and every day the stress was taking its toll on me. I couldn't find joy in anything in my life. I was fearful that everything I had worked for my entire life was going up in smoke.

Days felt like weeks, weeks felt like months, and months felt like years. I had a time towards the end where I didn't sleep for about five days. I would try and lie down at night but my mind wouldn't shut off. So I would get up and go back to the office shutting the doors behind me. I was doing everything humanly possible to save my fortune, but it was getting away from me and the economy and financial markets were out of control.

I was stunned at the thought of losing everything. I was not giving up. I was going to fight to the end. I couldn't sleep or eat. I was on lock down in my office when suddenly the doors flew open.

"Todd, it's time to let this go!" Erica yelled. "It's been five days of you not sleeping or eating and stressing about this nonstop. If you don't stop this now, you will probably have a heart attack and die." Her tone was insistent and serious, as if she had been sitting on these words for a while now. She continued, "I don't care if we lose all the money! We will be all right! We don't need the money; we need you around! We have each other. We're all healthy. THAT is what matters!"

Everything that I had been fighting for in this market crash, the ego of being a multi-millionaire business tycoon after my baseball career, the freedom that all the money had provided for my family, all seemed very meaningless after those courageous and loving words from my wife. During these turbulent economic times, some the wealthiest people in the country were falling and their families were falling apart as well. Many of our friends were getting divorced. Money can cover up a lot of things, and when it's gone people's true colors tend to come out.

My wife's true colors were absolutely radiant in our darkest hour. She was strong and firm and willing to fight for our family and pull me out of a destructive cycle. We were both at the "Decision Time." She had decided it was time to fight for our family and to save what we could of the life we had built. I decided to swallow my pride and listen to her. I knew she was right—my family needed me around, and we needed each other, regardless of how many zeros we had to our name at the end of each devastating day.

The crash hit me extremely hard on a deeply personal level because for the first time in my life since Jason, I had failed. Just like when I was watching Jason's body reject my bone marrow, I sat watching my fortune disintegrate and wishing there was something I could do. I felt completely helpless and lost and I had no hope. I felt like a failure. I had lost sight of the life-saving lesson I talked about in the introduction—I had given my mind to my circumstances, and I was allowing my enemy to fully consume me. I was out of control and it was painful, embarrassing, and angering. Erica's words that day reminded me that my identity is not in my successes or failures. She reminded me that I was loved and needed regardless of what came of our finances. I desperately needed that reminder. My decision time came in that moment when I had to choose to humble myself, listen to my wife, honor her voice in my life and trust the wisdom she was giving me. I had to decide to take back the parts of my mind that I had given over to this situation, regardless of how the rest of it played out.

I stayed in the markets until the bitter end. My entire fortune came down to within days, hours, and maybe even minutes of the bottom. I owned thousands of shares of Apple and it was now gone. Apple went from the 80s to over 500 on the rebound. I had no one to blame. I borrowed the money I had invested and my loans were called so I was sold out. I was playing with fire and I got burned. Leverage is very dangerous when not used responsibly. I call it the devil. If I would have never used the amount of leverage that I did, then I would never have felt the crash of 2007-2009 the way I did. I certainly wouldn't have been wiped out of the security markets, and if I had not been leveraged out of the market, my security accounts would be worth more than $40 million today.

I'm grateful for those difficult times in business and in the markets. I'm grateful for the pain that I went through. I'm grateful for my rise and for my fall because I learned. I made the decision to learn from everything I experienced. I made the decision to never again leverage my success in a way that threatens to put me in a position where I could lose it all. I lost money, but I gained a needed perspective of what life is like at rock bottom. Losing the money allowed me to improve my Peak Performance method because hitting the bottom gave me the needed perspective and opportunity to fully experience the rollercoaster of being a peak performer. When you play big and strive to live world class, you will either win big or lose big. I have experienced both. It is my hope that I lost big so that you don't have to, but if losing big is part of your story, I want you to know that you are not alone. Over the last six years, I have been blessed to build a business all over North America and globally. I have been building my empire back one asset at a time, with my greatest asset of all being my beautiful family.

My success came when I reached "Decision Time," I refined my goals for my current season. I re-strategized and found where my passion and need intersected. When you're at your lowest low and feeling hopeless, it's difficult to take your mind off your circumstances long enough to fight to get free from them. This becomes a vicious cycle if you don't engage during decision time and refine your goals. When you can re-discover even a small spark of passion, you can succeed again.

The most inspiring success stories come one step after the darkest hour. There's a reason so many stories have the same plot of the hero prevailing after pushing through their rock bottom—because we can all connect to that. Like my financial hit, your lowest low may seem to continue for years. Or when you thought you were at rock bottom, something else may have happened that buried you deeper than you thought possible. When you make the decision to fight for your world class life and be a peak performer, even in your darkest hour you *will* win. Knowing you will win gives you the fire to keep searching for the open door to your success. Or it gives you the belief in yourself to carve out your own exit if there are no doors in sight. Have you ever noticed how every lost thing is always found in the very last place you look? Do you want to know why that is? Because once you've found it, you stop looking for it. So, while you're searching for a way out, just know it will be in the last place you look. The only way to find it is to keep looking. Once you find it, you can stop looking and start pursuing your next goals.

It is important to notice that I did not overcome this alone. In this story, it was Erica who worked alongside me to pull me off the wall and bring me into my decision time. At every critical crossroad and decision time, there have been working partners and mentors who have guided and counseled me along the way.

CHAPTER 7

STEP 7 – WORKING PARTNERS

ONE THING I'VE learned through every high and low in my journey towards living world class is that you cannot succeed in isolation. Your success and your ability to be a peak performer are dependent on your willingness to surround yourself with the right people. The people you choose to surround yourself with are vital to your success. I call these people working partners.

Living world class requires you to surround yourself with other world class people who are experiencing the success that you want, or who have the expertise in areas you lack. Your success is dependent on the wisdom and knowledge these people carry. Your working partners can be friends, mentors, business partners—anyone whose opinion you value enough to listen to, even when you don't fully understand their reasoning. Sometimes this takes the shape of an obvious partnership. For example, in the last chapter, I talked about my wife Erica playing an essential role in pulling me out of self-destruct mode and getting my head on straight to fight our way out of our financial crises. In that situation, as in countless other times throughout our marriage, she was my working partner.

So, what exactly is a working partner? It's someone whom you have given license to speak into your life in one way or another. This can be encouragement, correction, coaching, advice, or any other form of helping you work through difficulties or triumphs. Typically, it is someone you trust and are willing to listen to. Often, it is someone who you recognize holds a valuable insight and perspective that you are blind to. Your working partners cover your blind spots and are equally committed to seeing you succeed. A healthy set of working partnerships should be an amalgamation of reciprocal and one-sided partners.

Reciprocal Working Partners

In reciprocal working partnerships—such as a marriage, friendship, or business partnership—both parties are equally committed to the results because both parties are impacted by the results. These partners are personally invested in your success on a deep and often inseparable level. Your success is their success. This creates a strong partnership because there is instant comradery. You are in the trenches together, sharing your unique perspectives and sharpening each other's skills and expertise. You recognize that you each carry a different set of strengths and weaknesses, and you value those differences in a way that makes you open to learning from that reciprocal working partner. You both learn from each other, improving each other's chances for success, and walking alongside one another from start to finish.

One-Sided Working Partners

One-sided working partners are a bit more difficult to define. These are the people who will indirectly benefit from your success. They are committed to your success, but you are not obligated to return the favor. Even if your success might indirectly increase their success, you have the freedom to focus on yourself. These are commonly referred to as mentors, but the definition goes beyond that. For example, these can be mentors, coaches, bosses, or teachers. These people are still committed to walking alongside you in your pursuit of success, but it is often their job to do so.

While one-sided working partners may become friends along the way, their primary job is to help you succeed. These are the people you are likely paying to learn from. They have a clear expertise that will benefit you, and you know that the main goal is to learn from them. The beauty of one-sided working partners is they have a degree of authority that merits respect. They have the freedom to be more direct and can dish out more tough-love than your reciprocal partners. Their brutal honesty doesn't threaten the relationship and doesn't pose a risk to their own success. There is a mutual understanding that you are there to learn from them, you want to be there, you trust their methods, and are ready to learn and follow their process. Some one-sided partnerships might be a short, goal-oriented relationship that ends when the goal is accomplished, while others might have more long-term involvement in your life and overall success.

I'm going to walk you through some personal examples of these various working partnerships in my life and career. As I mentioned before, my early career was fraught with my inability to control my emotions on the field. If the game wasn't going well, I was a ticking time bomb and everyone knew it. I was fiery and passionate, but I was volatile. A few missteps and my game was completely derailed. The whole stadium could sense my frustration, especially the opposing hitters. I would agonize over prior mistakes I had no control over rather than focusing on what I had to do next. Opposing hitters feed off a pitcher who is not in control. The pitcher's frustration gives them confidence that, at any moment, they can get the best of him. My father noticed this pattern early in my career and encouraged me to study other pitchers' on-field demeanor. He suggested I watch Dave Stewart, who pitched for the Oakland Athletics. Dad said, "When Dave is pitching you can't tell if he is winning or losing the game. His expressions never change and he looks like he is always in control."

I watched Dave closely over the years and Dad was right; Dave was always in control. Dave Stewart won 20 games in four consecutive years with the Oakland Athletics and I greatly admired him as a pitcher. In 1993, we became teammates on the Toronto Blue Jays. I knew I wanted to be mentored by him and learn directly from his methods and process. It was an added blessing to become reciprocal working partners with the guy whose career I had been studying for years! He was an incredible mentor and I looked up to him because of everything he had accomplished in the game as a starting pitcher. He was a natural leader and mentor, even just as a friend. Wisdom poured out of him at every turn. I quickly learned he was in control of every aspect of his life; he was in the zone on and off the field.

Our first day together in spring training he asked me if I wanted to go for a run after our workout. I jumped at the opportunity. I was going running with my new mentor, all-star pitcher and 20-game winner Dave Stewart. We changed into our shorts and running shoes and hit the streets, running all over Dunedin, Florida. We ran with no end in sight for what seemed like an eternity. All I could think was, "How much further are we going to go?" We ran in silence, one foot in front of the other.

Finally, I could see the ballpark and our first run together was coming to an end. I was so relieved. As we entered the stadium, Dave asked, "So what'd you think about on the run?"

I looked at him. "Honestly, all I could think about was how far we were going to run." Dave let out a genuine deep belly laugh, signaling that my honesty was appreciated but we had a lot of work to do. I then asked Dave, "What did you think about?"

He answered confidently, "I was throwing perfect pitches in my head during the entire run." I was in awe of his focus and vision for the season from day one. While I let my mind be clouded with my circumstance and discomfort, wanting to solve the unknown questions that were out of my control, he was using his mental space to improve his game and visualize throwing perfect pitches. At that moment, I saw what separated us. I saw what it took to be an all-star pitcher, and I wanted the focus and drive that Dave had. I was even more ready to learn from him.

A week later, Dave asked, "What kind of a season are you going to have?" Without hesitation, he continued, "Because I'm going to have a great year!" He knew I was taken off guard by his question, but these were the things he always had on his mind. I had every intention of having a great year, but I hadn't verbalized and meditated on it the way Dave had, and his resolve to succeed bled through every aspect of his life. I was blown away by his mindset.

I hung on to every word as Dave continued talking, "You know Todd, every fan of our club that watches our games either in person or on TV is counting on us as starting pitchers to be the best that we can be on game day. Every person that works for the organization, including every person that works at the stadium while the game is going on, is counting on us. The owners of the club who are paying our salaries are counting on us. The entire scouting department and front office staff who work for our organization are counting on us. The general manager who selected us to be starting pitchers on this team is counting on us. The manager and the coaching staff, everyone who is wearing the same uniform, are counting on us to do our job and give our team the best chance to win the game. The trainers and team doctors who keep us healthy are counting on us. Every teammate going through the same sacrifice of fighting for the world championship is counting on us to be at our best. And, last but not least, our families are counting on us to provide for them through this game. That is what you have to remember when you think of your role as starting pitcher."

When Dave finished, I was in total shock. I had never thought of it that way, but he was totally right. That conversation changed the way I prepared for every game.

I prepared for every start like it was my last. I took the responsibility seriously. I conditioned myself with the mentality of leaving it all on the field every time the manager gave me the ball as starting pitcher. The game and our team were bigger than me. Because Dave recognized the gravity of his role as starting pitcher, he was willing to be a reciprocal working partner with me and the rest of his teammates. He recognized that his success was our success and vice versa. He was the epitome of a team player. He was committed to our team's success by being fully engaged and in the zone on his own success. But, he was also committed to helping me become the best player that I could be because he recognized that this team was bigger than himself.

Imagine taking on your job, your company, or your life with the same mindset that Dave Stewart had about his job as a starting pitcher. Imagine taking on the responsibility of every choice, action, thought, response, emotion, and decision in your life right now and putting it into perspective with the people who are partnered with your success, directly and indirectly. As I mentioned in the introductory chapter, Dave quickly became a close friend whom I gave full permission to speak into my life and influence my decisions. I knew with his wisdom, dedication, and determination I could trust his influence over me. He had achieved what I hoped to, and he had a consistency on and off the field that I aspired to achieve.

He was unshakeable. Dave was right; our team did have a great season and we won the World Series that year.

Despite our team's success in 1993, I personally had an average season and pitched very poorly in the World Series. After a year of shadowing and learning from Dave, I was hungry to transform my life and deal with my past hurts, which were manifesting in my pitching. I was ready to position myself to have the mindset of a peak performer like Dave. I knew I would need a one-sided working partner who could help me gain the freedom I needed. I had heard the name Harvey Dorfman thrown around by other players. Harvey was a renowned mental skills coach and sports psychologist known for taking top players' careers to the next level. I called Dave. When he answered the phone, I said, "Tell me the first thing that comes to mind when I say the name Harvey Dorfman." Without hesitation, Dave said, "Go see him." Immediately after hanging up with Dave, I dialed Harvey's number and booked a time to meet with him.

Harvey was the mentor with whom I spent 12 consecutive hours in a hotel room, processing through the various hurts and disappointments that made me lose control on the field. He is the one who issued the life-changing challenge that I mentioned in the introductory chapter: to stay in control of my mind and emotions for seven days. In our time together he told me, "People can take your body, but only you can give them your mind." It was putting those words immediately into play that stopped me from fighting back when Dave and I were wrongfully beaten and arrested. It saved us from being guilty in that situation, and I can't imagine what would have happened if I hadn't reached out for Harvey's expertise when I did.

Harvey was the perfect example of a one-sided working partner who was in my life for a short season, but vital to my success. He was committed to my success from the beginning to the end of our time together. He was committed to holding me accountable and celebrating my victories with me as I walked through the process of regaining control over my mind and my life. I knew that I needed his expertise at that phase of my life and I was willing to do whatever it took to get it. Your working partners will help you climb out of the ditch when you're faced with decision time. Dave helped me realize that I was not yet performing at my peak, and Harvey's expertise gave me the necessary tools to get there.

Being coachable and willing to be mentored by others is an invaluable key to your success. Being coached came naturally to me because of my baseball career. When I went into the business world, the first thing I did was search out the peak performers. I took them to lunch to find out what I could learn from them to mirror their success. In everything I have attempted, I have always sought the experts in that field. If you're striving for greatness, you need to be able to learn from those who are already successful in what you want to achieve or those who have led others to success. Most successful people are more than willing to give back to people in their field. People are eager and excited about sharing their knowledge and expertise. If you don't have access to meet with those people in person, you can always read their books and listen to their audios, seeking the voices of those who have created greatness in their field. Learning from mentors and coaches is the first step, but following through on their advice and putting your knowledge into action is what creates peak performers.

I am a big fan of the teachings of the late Jim Rohn. I have his audio series, *The Challenge to Succeed*, in my car. They have been in my car for 18 months straight and when I'm driving, they're playing. I have turned my car into a mobile university for success. You may be wondering why I have listened to the same audios for 18 months. I want to listen to them over and over until I become those audios. The greatest reward in the world is that my 11-year-old son loves to listen to them with me. Imagine what that is doing for his life at such a young and impressionable age. In just one of his wise insights, Rohn offers a valuable lesson about the partners you choose for your life, "You must constantly ask yourself these questions: Who am I around? What are they doing to me? What have they got me reading? What have they got me saying? Where do they have me going?

What do they have me thinking? And most important, what do they have me becoming? Then ask yourself the big question: Is that okay?"

Success and greatness are a collection of thoughts and ideas from many sources of expertise poured into a person or company who puts those thoughts into action. It's the very reason why most, if not all, of the wealthiest people have mentors, coaches, and mastermind groups. Watching the Olympics, you'll see this same reality very blatantly play out. After every athlete is finished with their performance, the first person they see and talk to is their coach, who is right there on the sidelines. The greatest athletes in the world all have coaches. That coach's ability is what makes the athletes great.

I have benefitted countless times from working alongside legendary coaches who were willing to teach me and walk alongside me step-by-step until I could execute the plays on my own. It's human nature to want great results, and working partners multiply your results. It's vital to have someone who shares in your vision, holds you accountable for every action you take or don't take towards your goals, and provides a perspective other than your own with complete honesty.

In 1995 I joined the Oakland Athletics after spending seven seasons with the Toronto Blue Jays. I was sad to leave Toronto, but I was excited to be joining my new team. I was especially excited to get to work with their pitching coach Dave Duncan. After seven years, I was still not pitching consistently and I knew I was not performing at my peak. Dave Duncan had a knack for taking guys at a plateau in their careers and making them explosive pitchers. My first two starts with the A's were subpar. Sitting with me after my workout, Dave Duncan asked, "Hey, why don't you throw more curveballs in the game?" I told him that the Blue Jays had told me for seven years that I needed to throw more curveballs. Dave then said, "Todd if you have a major league curveball, it will allow you to throw fewer sliders, which are your out pitch. If you throw fewer sliders, your pitching would be more effective and you would dominate."

To understand his advice, it helps to know that both a curveball and a slider are breaking pitches. A curveball has a higher arch and is an off-speed pitch. A slider is closer to the speed of a fastball. Basically, I was throwing all fastballs and sliders in the game, which allowed major league hitters to time the ball better because every pitch was high-speed. If I were to throw more curveballs, it would keep the hitters off balance. The problem was that because my slider developed into a great pitch over the years, I had lost confidence in my curveball because I didn't feel it was as effective. The result was that I stopped throwing curveballs or threw them on a very limited basis and I had become a two-pitch pony. The second problem was I wasn't sure how to use my curveball in the game effectively to set up my fastball and slider, and it was humbling to admit this to my new pitching coach. Dave Duncan said, "I have an idea! How about if I call all the curveballs that I think you should throw in the next game, so you don't have to think about when to throw them?" I trusted Dave and his reputation of helping major league pitchers take their careers to the next level. I agreed to let him call all the curveballs in my next start.

Three days later it was time for me to take the mound against the Minnesota Twins in the Metrodome. The Twins were a great club at home and the Metrodome was a nightmare to pitch in. Before the game, I got together with Dave Duncan and my all-star catcher Terry Steinbach. We went over the game plan of how we were going to attack the Twins' hitters. Right before the meeting broke, Dave said to Terry, "Also, I will be calling all the curveballs tonight, so look into the dugout after every pitch." My agreement was that every time I got the sign to throw a curveball, I would throw it with all my might. That night, I struck out 10 hitters and got the win against the Twins. I couldn't believe it. In seven previous seasons, I had never struck out 10 batters in one game. I was so excited; I had a new toy and it was called a curveball.

I hugged Dave after the game, "So will you call all the curveballs in my next game too?"

He looked at me and smiled. "I will help you with when to throw curveballs until you feel comfortable doing it on your own." My new pitching coach had become my working partner and my results were starting to show the value in our partnership. I ended the season with 14 wins and seven losses, even though the club finished in last place that year. I also went on to strike out 10 or more hitters in 10 different games that year, finishing second in the American League in strikeouts behind Randy Johnson, and for the first time in my career striking out more than 200 batters in a single season! I had exploded my results by having a working partner. The second half of my career looked a lot different than my first half. Working with Dave Duncan helped me become a well-rounded pitcher and our time together made me a legitimate strikeout pitcher, striking out over 200 hitters in a season a few more times in my career!

A working partner or accountability partner is not someone who tells you what to do. They are someone who works with you, shares in your vision, goals, and work ethic, and multiplies your results. Dave Duncan didn't just tell me what to do; he helped me do it until I could do it alone. He was a true working partner. If your working partner is not locking arms and doing the work with you, then I would suggest it's time to find a new partner. Your partner should be adding energy and resources to the direction you want to go. He or she should be completely bought into the vision. Your partner should be willing to go through the sacrifice of pursuing greatness with you and have a no-quit attitude.

If you are not where you want to be right now, it's time to critically analyze the working partnerships in which you have placed yourself. Do you have both reciprocal and one-sided working partners that have the same vision and desire for your success as you do? While there are certainly some gray areas between reciprocal and one-sided working partnerships, and most likely a third "in between" category, the general separations stand.

Reciprocal working partners are committed to your success based on mutual benefit and operate more as a teammate. You are equally invested in the success of your reciprocal working partners, and often help them pursue their dreams simultaneously. One-sided working partners are committed to your success because it is their job to help you and they are indirectly impacted by your success. In both cases, you want people who care about you and value your success. You want people who have the results or the expertise that you would like to master in your own life. Ultimately, you want people who are willing to follow through and work alongside you until your goals are complete.

One of my favorite examples of working partners is draft horses. A draft is massive, bred to be a working animal. In the early days, farmers used them for pulling heavy objects and plowing fields. The animals weigh thousands of pounds and are very muscular, making them ideal for pulling. A single draft horse can pull up to eight thousand pounds. Naturally, people assumed putting two draft horses together would double the weight they could pull, making them capable of pulling 16 thousand pounds together. But when two draft horses are working together they can pull up to 24 thousand pounds. This working partnership doesn't double the results, it triples them! But the analogy runs even deeper because if two draft horses work and train together over time, the partnership that could once pull 24 thousand pounds can now pull 32 thousand pounds. That means that from learning to work together, each horse doubles their original ability by working in a cohesive and well-trained team. If that's what horses are capable of accomplishing as a team, on a strictly physical level, imagine what humans can accomplish and learn from working together!

Exercise

Who are the people in your life whose influence you deeply value? Who do you need to be more intentional with to establish a clearly defined working partnership? Who in your life is already a working partner and how has that helped you? Who are people you imagine you would work well with, that you want to reach out to and start forming a working partnership? Take some time to critically analyze your current or desired working partnerships in the tables below.

Reciprocal Working Partners

Name	Relationship	Shared Vision	Action Steps Towards Success
Ex: Dave Stewart	Teammate / Mentor	Be World Class MLB Pitchers	Daily Training Together / Friendship / Accountability

One-Sided Working Partners

It is great if your one-sided partnerships are real people you get to work with directly (such as coaches, teachers, mentors) but these could also be books, seminars, or other inaccessible people you hope to learn from.

Name	Relationship	What You Hope to Learn	How You Will Learn
Ex: Harvey Dorfman	Mental Skills Coach	Stay In Control On The Field	12-hour One-on-One Session with Follow-up

CHAPTER 8

STEP 8 - TAKE THE QUIT OPTION OFF THE TABLE

WE'VE NOW REACHED what I believe is one of the most important steps in the Peak Performance method—Take the Quit Option Off the Table! Honestly, this is both a first step and an ongoing step. When you start, you must decide that "quit" isn't in your vocabulary. It's way easier said than done! No one starts a goal with the intention of quitting. That's why it's an ongoing part of the process toward living world class.

You must decide that divorcing from your dreams and goals is not an option. Ever. If you internalize that choice, and when the thought of quitting dances through your mind along the way, you won't even entertain it. If quitting is truly off the table at all times, it's not even worth a "what if" or a backup plan. When the going gets tough, you can absolutely re-strategize, figuring out what areas you need to strengthen and where you need to ask for help, but walking away is never part of the equation. Reaching your full potential will be a constant battle. Someone who has never struggled is someone who has never won. If you are going through struggles, fighting endlessly to achieve your goals, then you are probably right on track for success. Every setback is a setup. Every battle scar builds your endurance and your strength. You are earning compound interest on the time and energy that you invest in your dreams. Every time you fall, you are learning. You are getting better. You are gaining wisdom.

Failure and quitting should not go hand-in-hand. The key is getting back up every time. Og Mandino said it best, "I will persist until I succeed. The prizes of life are at the end of each journey, not near the beginning; and it is not given to me to know how many steps are necessary in order to reach my goal. Failure I may still encounter at the thousandth step, yet success hides behind the next bend in the road. Never will I know how close it lies unless I turn the corner."

Turning the corner is the key. It blows my mind how many people quit mere inches away from success. We never know when we are inches from success, so we tend to base how close we are on how far we've come. We draw our conclusions from a mix of prior experience and our misguided perceptions of how quickly we've seen others succeed. We may convince ourselves success is inches away because we've been grinding on this goal for years. Then, when life throws new curve balls, we get discouraged and assume success must not be possible.

We think back to how effortlessly and quickly we saw someone else succeed. The issue is the snapshots we see of other people's lives and success is no indication of how much they've sacrificed to get to where they are. Sure, that friend might have graduated from university with his dream job locked down, spent the rest of his career climbing the corporate ladder, and now sits at the peak of success. Maybe from an outside perspective, it seems he's never struggled; his success was handed to him quickly and he's had an easy life riding that wave. But you never saw the sacrifices and choices he made towards that goal from childhood! Even if you were friends, you might not have seen the times he decided to study instead of watching TV, the times he decided to read a book related to his future goals instead of play a video game, the parties he didn't go to. These little sacrifices and the commitment to his goals led him to achieve what you now perceive as effortless success. No doubt there were times he wanted to quit but decided that was not an option—both in his career and the years leading up to it. There's no cut-and-dried timeline on success. You aren't guaranteed to succeed after a certain amount of years, so you must decide to take the quit option off the table!

When the quit option is off the table, you are relentlessly committed to seeing your goal realized. You will stick it out and turn that next corner to find out if you were inches away, or if there's another corner up ahead. Then you will walk to that next corner and repeat the process! Because quitting isn't an option, you will find out where your success lies as you pursue your dreams. Success plays hide-and-seek with us. It gives us glimpses of where it's hiding that keep us going, knowing we are close. When you feel like you've fully searched one room, you move on to the next…if it's not found in that room, you might circle back to the first and dig deeper, or you might move on to the next new room. The key is always taking the next step and continuing to search.

As promised, I want to circle back to the story I told in Chapter 4. As a quick re-cap, I had just spent the entire off-season of 1987 training like never before. This paid off in spring training and I finally made the Toronto Blue Jays' major league team. My dream was short lived and I was pushed back down to the minors' triple A team in August. I dominated my game in triple A and was brought back up to the major league team in September 1988, where I finished out the season with minimal playing time. Since I had proven myself and worked my way back up to the major leagues, I thought I was set. The Blue Jays' general manager, Pat Gillick, then told me that I needed to spend the 1988 winter season playing winter ball in Venezuela and learning how to throw a slider, or I wouldn't make the major league club in 1989. So I put aside my anger and frustration at the situation and decided to make the sacrifice. For the second year in a row, I was giving up my rest and recuperation season for intensive training. I knew it would be worth it. I gave it my all, and in 1989 I made the Toronto Blue Jays' major league club once again!

I had taken the quit option off the table. I had put my goals in perspective with my "Why," I committed to this radical change of behaviors, and I was willing to make the sacrifice and push past the enemy in my mind that was saying it wouldn't be worth it. I had decided that I was going to succeed in securing my spot in the MLB not just for this season but for years to come. My working partners and mentors were on board with my process, and I had earned the right to my spot on that team. I had followed my Peak Performance method to a T and was now experiencing the success that was guaranteed at the end of sticking to the process with relentless devotion! Except, real life doesn't always work out that smoothly. I did make the team, but that doesn't mean my resolve wasn't going to be tested.

After sacrificing my winter to master the game, I was confident in how I had developed as a player. I was once again living my dream of being an MLB pitcher. But I got too comfortable with the taste of what I believed was promised and deserved success. I was performing averagely—I wasn't pitching poorly but I wasn't pitching excellently either. In May of 1989, I was once again pushed down to the minor leagues. I knew I wasn't performing at my peak, but I still took this decision extremely personally. In my mind, the demotion was without merit. I stormed out of the locker room shaking with frustrated rage. I understood the last year, but now? I had spent my time during winter ball working on gaining the consistency and new skills that were previously lacking. I belonged in the major leagues. In my arrogance, I truly believed that I was performing at a major league level and felt I was the best I had ever been! I knew there was room for improvement, but nothing that more time on the major league field couldn't fix. In my anger, I did what anyone one else would if they had a major league pitching coach on speed dial—I called my dad. I wanted him to comfort and confirm to me that the Blue Jays had made a fatal error and were completely unmerited in pushing me down.

At the time, my dad was the pitching coach for the New York Mets. When he answered, I explained the situation through gritted teeth and clenched fists. I vented all of my complaints and frustrations about being pushed back again. I closed my rant with a winning line, "Canada is a hockey country. They clearly don't know shit about baseball!" I took a deep breath, catching up on the air I forgotten to take in throughout this rant, waiting for my dad to echo my sentiments.

His even and strong tone cut through the pause, "You know Todd, I'd love to have you on my pitching staff here in New York."

"I know! That'd be aweso –"

"But *not* the way you're pitching now!" he cut me off, with stern resolve. His words pierced me. He broke my stunned silence by continuing, "You're not pitching anywhere near your capabilities. I know what you're capable of, and you're not there yet."

His words were the last thing I wanted to hear in that moment. What I didn't recognize at the time was his words were exactly what I needed. Instead of taking his words to heart I sheepishly replied, "So…can I talk to mom now?" knowing that she would echo my hurt rather than kick me while I was down. I knew Dad was right. I knew I was capable of more. But in that setback, after already being sent down the previous year, I just wanted to blame the club and throw in the towel rather than take responsibility and keep working towards performing at my peak. I was looking for someone to agree with me, but my dad had the strength to call me higher, to make me recognize my role in this situation, and realize that I could still overcome this setback. He reminded me that the quit option was off the table—I was better than this, and I would overcome it!

Hanging up the phone, I packed up my apartment and prepared my mind for the drive to Syracuse to join the Blue Jays' minor league team. I didn't want to go, and it was late, but I drove through the night because I was too upset to sleep, and I didn't want to risk changing my mind. The toughest battle of my career was playing out in my thoughts as I drove. It was a lonely drive, and for the first time in my life, I questioned if I was going to be able to live out my dream. After all, I wasn't my father.

As countless people reminded me over the years, I wasn't even *like* my father. Maybe those people were right? What am I going to do next if baseball doesn't work out? Maybe I should spare myself the embarrassment of not making it and just quit now. I was extremely vulnerable. I was beaten down and frustrated. I felt hopeless. But, I was still driving. Every mile marker I passed on that drive signaled that no matter what I was fighting in my mind, I was still moving towards my goal. I was driving to my new city, my new team, my new season. As frustrated as I was, I was still on my way to face my disappointment head on. Slowly, the dark cover of nightfall softened into dawn and the orange glow of the sunrise began to illuminate the sky.

Shifting from dark to light, the world around me began to wake up and I knew I needed to do the same. "The sun will *still* come up tomorrow." My dad's words resounded through my spirit, silencing my doubts and fears. He always quoted this phrase as a reminder that no matter how hard life gets, it goes on. We have no way to stop life from moving forward. We have to face the next day; we have to choose how to use that time. We can't escape it. Loneliness faded into the background and I rededicated myself to my dreams of being an MLB pitcher. I was going to be all in no matter what. If that meant being the best damn pitcher the minor league has ever seen, then that's what I was going to be. I was not going to let a momentary setback cause me to hang up my glove when success had never been closer. Sure, I had made the major leagues before, but I was not my best, and I finally was willing to recognize that this setback was giving me the chance to become the best pitcher that I could be. If I was going to fail, then I was going to give the world a front row seat. I didn't care what others thought. I had a job to do and a dream to accomplish, and I finally had the resolve to do it.

No matter what came my way that season, I refused to quit. Quitting was once again off the table. I re-committed to being the first one to the ballpark and the last one to leave every day. I knew what it took to become the best; I'd worked my way out of this ditch before and I intended to do it again. I didn't want to stay where I was, but I was committed to making the most of it so I would be prepared for my imminent success.

One month later I was called back to Toronto to rejoin the major league team. One month. That setback made me into the player I needed to be. It was a wake-up call realizing that I was one setback away from allowing my mind to reach extreme hopelessness. I knew I needed to be stronger than that going forward. I knew that quitting could no longer be an option no matter what the road ahead brought. Leaving Syracuse, I vowed that I was never coming back to the minor leagues again. I started 12 games during the second half of that season for Toronto, pitched game two of the playoffs against the Oakland Athletics and became the youngest starter in Blue Jays' history to pitch a playoff game. That was the true beginning of my 15-season MLB career that landed me on three world championship teams.

I am constantly struck with the thought, "What if I had quit that night?" In the moment, I felt like being pushed back to the minors for the second year in a row was the league's way of saying I would never make it. In reality, I had never been closer to achieving my dream. My dad, and the managers, all saw that I was capable of more and they wouldn't settle for less! It felt like my dreams were miles away on that drive when in reality it was just one more corner and one more month before I fulfilled and sustained my life-long goal! When you feel like entertaining the thought of quitting, ask yourself this, "What if I knew my success was one month away?" Then give it your all for that month and work harder than you've ever worked before. If your breakthrough doesn't come by the end of that month, guess what? You're now one month closer to your success than you've ever been before and what if your success is *now* just a month away?

Quitting is the only thing that guarantees failure. Everything else is getting you closer to success than you've ever been before. Even if you've experienced your desired success in the past, you are closer now to the world class life than you were at your last peak. Do you know why? Because now you have a foundation, you know what it takes to succeed, you know you can make it, and you will experience a new level of success that is far beyond the previous achievements. You can be thankful when you face suffering and setbacks because it's building your character to handle more success. As my favorite Bible verse says, "…we rejoice in our sufferings, knowing that suffering produces endurance, and endurance produces character, and character produces hope…" (Rom 5:3-4 ESV). Changing my mindset to appreciate the suffering I was facing allowed me to regain my hope. That hope kept me fighting for my dreams and goals. The days when your body aches, your desire is low, and you are exhausted, are the days you need to take the next step.

Giving up is the cop-out decision when things get tough. All great success stories are about persisting through the difficult times. The people or companies that inspire me the most are the ones that found a way to keep their dreams alive. The ones who continued to sacrifice even though they had very little short-term success. The ones who inspired the masses didn't take the easy option of quitting; they continued to focus on their goals in the middle of a crisis, hanging on with everything they had. Every day you are writing your own success story. When you get to the end of your life what will people say about you? Be known as someone who refuses to quit, who believes everything is possible, and who works hard to achieve your success. Be the person who others turn to in their difficult situations as a pillar of strength, wisdom, and assurance that there is hope at the end of the struggle. Be someone who always gets up, no matter how many times you get knocked down. Be the person who always finds a way to take one more seemingly impossible step. Ultimately, be a peak performer against all odds because you decided to take the quit option off the table.

The great Muhammad Ali once said, "I hated every minute of training, but I said, 'Don't quit. Suffer now, and live the rest of your life as a champion.'" If you are suffering now, keep going. The champion inside you is being sculpted. Your success story is being written so you can live the life you deserve and be an example. You will inspire others with your persistence, and empower them to find the champion in themselves. I can promise you this: if you don't quit you *will* win!

CHAPTER 9

STEP 9 - WORK IT AND LIVE IT!

CONGRATULATIONS! YOU'VE MADE it to the final chapter and the final, and most rewarding, step in the Peak Performance method—working and living your success. Before we unpack what this looks like, let's look at what we've done to get to the place where living your success can be possible!

Step 1 – Setting Goals

Returning to the childlike mentality where big dreams are possible, you took the time to clarify your vision, identify your top 3 - 5 goals for this year, and make a plan. Setting goals allows you to make a plan that can carry you through any rough patches along your journey to success. Rather than allowing your hopes and dreams to remain a distant "maybe," setting your goals brings them into reality by initiating a plan of action so you can see your dreams through to completion.

Step 2 – New Behaviors

Based on your goals, you have identified which areas of your life need to be refined and strengthened. These areas will require developing new behaviors and changing small things you do daily to help you become the person you want to be and achieve the success you want to achieve. By raising the level of excellence in the fundamental behaviors and character traits that you already possess, and introducing new behaviors that will work to help you gain qualities you were lacking, the level of everything that you do will grow exponentially.

Step 3 – The Why

Your "Why" is what will carry you far beyond anything else. It is the make or break of the Peak Performance method. Your "Why" must be two key things: clear and unshakeable. This can be based on the people or events that have shaped you, or the people your success will impact, but it is absolutely essential that your "Why" consistently stirs a level of passionate resolve in you that no person or circumstance could even threaten to remove. Your "Why" must be 100% irrevocable!.

Step 4 – Be Willing to Sacrifice

Success requires sacrifice. Those who live world class are those who are willing to give up short-term comforts for long-term gain. If you are willing to sacrifice, you are willing to do whatever it takes to become the person you need to be. You must maintain the perspective that major sacrifices made in some seasons will push you to reap the major rewards of your world class life!

Step 5 – Fighting the Enemy

Fighting the enemy is a defensive position in which you do whatever it takes to protect your mind from being derailed by the enemy. First, you identify your enemies and learn their strengths, weaknesses, and strategies. You have to know what you're up against. Enemies come in all shapes in sizes—other people, health setbacks, your own mindset, etc. You must use your enemies to fuel your resolve to succeed, rather than allowing them to derail your success. This is done by fully committing to the process and the fight whether that's mental or physical, and deciding that you WILL do whatever it takes to overcome whatever the enemy throws at you.

Step 6 – Decision Time

This step often goes hand-in-hand with facing challenges. When you've been grinding for success and still aren't seeing results, you are at a critical decision time. This is the time to press in, re-evaluate your goals if necessary, adjust your strategy, and decide to go all-in and not stop until your goal is completed. If your dream is still burning inside of you, it's time to fully commit! Find what's left of the fiery passion that initially drew you into this goal and pursue that whole-heartedly until it grows back into an unquenchable passion to succeed.

Step 7 – Working Partners

Next, it is absolutely essential to surround yourself with like-minded working partners who share in your goal and are equally invested in your success. These can either be reciprocal, such as a friend or teammate, or one-sided, such as a coach or mentor. Surround yourself with people who are willing to pour into you and invest in the vision that you have decided to pursue wholeheartedly. This is someone who can see from a perspective that might be a blind spot for you, who you have given permission to speak honestly into your life in order to help you succeed.

Step 8 – Take the Quit Option Off the Table

Quit cannot be in your vocabulary. You have to decide that no matter what happens, quitting is NOT an option. You have to keep in mind that the suffering you are experiencing isn't a reason to quit, but a reminder that you are closer to your success than you have ever been before. If you don't quit, you will succeed!

Step 9 – Work it and Live it

Once you have completed these first 8 steps, you are ready to experience step 9—Work it and Live it! Working and living your success is bittersweet because it is only the beginning of continuing to expand your horizon of success. While it is a major victory to get to this stage, it still requires dedication and hard work.

Success is a detailed plan of action followed through to the end. Success and failure are a matter of action or inaction. People who never succeed are those who lack the desire, vision, habits, mentors, and commitment. They are unwilling to make the necessary sacrifices to follow through on the process that creates success.

By this point in the book, I can guarantee you are not one of those people. Maybe you have had those tendencies in the past, but you have now made the decision to live world class. My method was designed to bring out the peak performer that is already in you. My goal is that by following my proven method, you will be released to live in your strengths and pursue your success with relentless devotion. The strategy for success may be simple but it's never going to be easy. To be the best in your field and to create greatness in your life, you are going to have to work hard. Here's my promise: it will be worth it. There are two key components to working and living your success—keep it simple and stay in the zone.

Jim Rohn said, "Success is neither magical nor mysterious. Success is the natural consequence of consistently applying basic fundamentals." In other words, you already have what it takes. The next step is effectively tapping into the peak performer inside you. Your peak performer starts out as an external persona, like crafting an avatar for a video game. The first 8 steps have built up the vision of what your peak performer looks like. This, in a way, is your idealized self. Some aspects of your peak performance identity are closer to your current reality than others, and that's OK. The important part is that your peak performer exists and there is clarity around the key elements—the goals, the behaviors, the "why," the correct mentality, and the working partners. There's a clear understanding of what it will take to win the game—willingness to sacrifice, fighting the enemies, deciding you can and will win, and removing the quit option. Your peak performer lives in this game; there is no reality for your peak performer outside of playing for your success. Your peak performer has one simple task—relentlessly pursue success. Slowly but surely, your core identity will merge with your peak performance identity until you have fully brought your peak performer to life. This happens by trusting the foundation that you've set for yourself with the Peak Performance method.

In 1992, my team, the Toronto Blue Jays, hit a rough patch. Our manager, Cito Gaston, called a team meeting before a game. Cito was a man who spoke with intentionality, so when he had something to say everyone paid close attention. He kept the message simple and said, "You guys have the talent to win this thing. There are only three things each one of you guys needs to understand: First, know what you are individually capable of. Second, know what your teammates are capable of. And third, know what your competition is capable of. If you master these three things—with the talent that we have in this locker room—we will be World Champions." His advice was simple and we all took it to heart and proved him right. That team went on to win the World Series in 1992 and in 1993. I will never forget that meeting. I have used that philosophy in every aspect of my life. So I challenge you to know yourself, know your team and know your competitors. That simple advice will always give you an edge.

Later in that 1992 season, I had just come off four

consecutive starts where I hadn't been pitching well. I had lost three of the four games. I felt like I was giving up hits even when I made good pitches. I was frustrated and our team needed me to pitch well because we were in the pennant race in August of 1992. I called my father who was currently the pitching coach for the New York Mets. Dad listened to me painstakingly describe every detail of my current struggle. Finally, when he could get a word in, he said, "First of all your mind is clouded with everything that you are thinking about. You have too much going on between your ears. When you go to the ballpark today, I want you to grab the baseball cap that you are going to pitch in and underneath the bill of the cap, I want you to write the word KISS in big bold letters. Every time you get into trouble on the mound I want you to take off your cap and look at that word."

I sat in silence for a minute and then questioned, "You want me to write the word KISS underneath the bill of my cap?"

Dad continued, "Yes, it stands for 'Keep it Simple Stupid.' You are making your job too hard by thinking about too many things. Keep the game simple. I want you to only think about a few things: stay back in your delivery and finish strong. In your mind, all I want you to think about is staying down with your pitches and attacking the strike zone. Let your defense do their part. I've seen a few clips of your starts on Sports Center and it looks like you're pitching up in the strike zone too much."

My next start was August 26, 1992, against the Chicago White Sox on their field. I had followed my father's instructions and written KISS underneath the bill of my game cap. Warming up in the bullpen I could hear Dad's words clearly—*stay back, finish strong and stay down in the strike zone.* I had a great warm up and I was ready to charge the mound with my renewed simplicity. I went into the eighth inning with a no-hitter, we were up nine to zero. Robin Ventura flew out to left on my first pitch to him. I needed five more outs for a no-hitter. The next hitter was Dan Pasqua and I got behind him with three balls and one strike. The next pitch I threw was middle of the zone and up and Pasqua hit a double into right center. I went on to get the next five outs, finishing the game with a one-hit shutout. It was the closest I ever got to pitching a no-hitter and it was all because I trusted my dad's advice to keep it simple.

I ended the season winning five of my last seven games and our team headed to the playoffs. My dad's advice to keep it simple and focus on a few basics made my pitching incredibly effective. Whether it's competing against the best athletes in the world, running your business, driving sales, or just simply wanting to get back into shape, success boils down to sticking to the simple things that you have mastered. It's not about doing more things, it's about becoming a master of a few key things.

When you have mastered the basics and everything that you need to do becomes second nature, it's time to get in the zone. When you are in the zone, the world around you goes silent and you are zeroed in on what you need to do. In this place, you are unstoppable. This is where keeping it simple and sticking to what you know empowers your peak performer to take center stage of your life. In the zone, your success practically works itself. You are on peak performance auto-pilot, sticking to the basics that are now ingrained in your identity. This position produces opportunities that you would not have had otherwise. Many times, the people you've surrounded yourself with— your working partners—will see your work ethic and drive and help make a way for you to succeed.

In Chapter 7 I mentioned Dave Duncan, my pitching coach on the Oakland Athletics who helped me overcome my pitching inconsistency and become a reliable strikeout pitcher. In 1996 Dave left Oakland and became the pitching coach for the St. Louis Cardinals. Dave had seen my dedication and drive over the years; he had helped me become the best that I could be and he knew that I could be trusted to play with a relentless drive to win. So, when the Cardinals' managers needed to add a reliable strikeout pitcher to their roster, Dave recommended they bring me on board. I was traded by the Oakland Athletics to the Cardinals and I was reunited with my friend and working partner! My integrity and identity as a peak performer were established and consistent, and the working partnership I developed with Dave opened this next opportunity for me. Once you've worked for your success and established your identity as a consistent peak performer, living it becomes easy. Your success begins to work itself because people are eager to work with you. They know what they are getting when they do so. It is these moments when you will fully experience being in the zone.

On October 1, 1996, I was pitching for the Cardinals against the San Diego Padres in game one of the National League Division Series. In the first inning, I had runners on first and third base and only one out. I started getting in my head, thinking about the runners who were already on base and getting frustrated that I had let them get there. Dave sensed my frustration and ran out to the mound to check in with me. My brain was scattered, focusing on the two runners on base, and the fact that the next batter was a legendary power hitter, Ken Caminiti—who was currently in his MVP season. I was focusing on the current circumstances that were out of my control, rather than dialing into the zone with a laser focus on my next pitch—the only thing I could control. Dave turned to me and said, "Look, Todd, you are one pitch away from ending this inning. Throw a good fastball down and away and get him to hit a double play." When Dave put it that way, an instant calm washed over me. I could make one good pitch, get the remaining two outs, and end this inning right now.

That was the push I needed to get back in the zone. It was no longer an overwhelming obstacle. It was just getting in the zone for one simple pitch. I let the world fade around me as I prepared for my next pitch. I zeroed in on what I needed to do in order to stay focused one pitch at a time. I retired Ken Caminiti by striking him out, and then got the next hitter, Wally Joyner, to ground-out to end the inning. I didn't get the groundball double play, but I managed to focus my game enough to end the inning with no runs.

Even when you get in the zone and apply the necessary laser-focus to the task at hand, things aren't always going to turn out perfectly. The key is that once you are in the zone, you have the focus to continue to adjust your approach and make the result the best that it can be with each twist and turn in the game plan. When you are in the zone, you are letting go of what you can't control in each moment and focusing on what's ahead of you. So, when the first pitch doesn't go as planned, you zone in on the next one and give it your all. What is done is out of your hands, and being in the zone is a constant forward-moving process. Our team went on to beat the Padres in all three games and claimed the NLDS championship!

When a situation doesn't go as you planned, your

success is not derailed. That is when you can get in the zone and try to release your mind from harboring and replaying the past. Entering the zone, you will realize the task in front of you provides limitless opportunities to succeed if you can figure out how to play it right. That one pitch might not have gone the way I wanted it to, but it didn't stop me from winning the inning, the game, and overall the championship. However, if I had let myself get out of the zone, it could have cost our team the entire game! I want to encourage you to get in the zone and stay in the zone. Let yourself press in with a laser focus on whatever is in front of you right now that you need to accomplish.

Being in the zone is an unchanged process for a peak performer. Whether I was zoning in to be the best that I could be during spring training drills, or zoning in on a pitch during a game-changing moment in a championship game, the focus was unchanged. In both scenarios, you must push away all external distractions. You must free yourself from the obligation of caring about things that are outside your momentary control. You have to keep it simple and stick to the basics that have become innate.

As a peak performer, you are offering to live in this zone in all seasons of your life. However, identifying the season you are in will help you structure what your zone will look like, and where you need to zero in your focus.

Because you are a peak performer, you likely have many goals, aspirations, and dreams.

Go back through the exercises and identify which ones seemed to be the most prominent as you worked through this book. This is your starting point. Next, you need to determine what season you are in. Is this a training season, where you have the time and energy to buckle down and drill yourself on new skills that will drive you to new heights of success? In the training season, you are building up the basics and growing holistically because you have the time to invest in overall improvements and skill development. It is in this training season that you are working closely with the teammates that you have around you. You are building up and strengthening those working partnerships and you are investing in the future by laying a firm foundation. Are you in the main season, where it's time to take the skills you have already built and finally channel them into your game? In the main season, you spend your time in the zone focusing on the next game. You tailor your preparations to your specific weaknesses that your next rival could exploit. Every moment is spent preparing for the next game on your calendar.

In this season, you are still working closely with your team but you have already established your roles and relationships, you are simply growing together and fine tuning the ways you work together. Or, are you in the post-season and championships? In the championships, you and your team know that you have what it takes to succeed; you wouldn't have made it this far if you didn't. It is now a process of trusting that each person will fulfill their role to the best of their abilities. This season is the culmination of the other two. In it, you will find times in which you go back to each previous season depending on what needs to be strengthened and addressed for continued success. Being in the zone may sometimes mean everyone focuses on performing individual tasks with precision and excellence. With this comes a necessary trust. You know who you are surrounded by, and you trust them to do their part with the same relentless drive that you have.

Identifying your season will shape how quickly you move through each step of the Peak Performance method, but no matter where you are, it is absolutely vital that you start immediately! As we conclude this book you must take a step back and look at all that you have discovered about yourself through these exercises and lessons:

What is your goal?

What are your new behaviors?

What is your "why?"

What sacrifices need to be made?

What enemies need to be taken down?

Have you decided to succeed?

Who are your working partners?

Is the quit option off the table?

Are you ready to work and live your success?

With these tools up your sleeve and a clear understanding of what season you are entering, it is time to get to work. The time is now! As I said at the very beginning of this book, I am extremely passionate about taking immediate action. My commitment to relentlessly pursuing success by taking immediate action saved my life and opened more opportunities than I could have ever dreamed. It is time to start pursuing your goals and your dreams. It is time to start living world class. It is time to become a peak performer. It is time to find relentless success!

ABOUT THE AUTHOR

Todd Stottlemyre, former right-handed starting pitcher in Major League Baseball, played 15 seasons for the Toronto Blue Jays, Oakland Athletics, St. Louis Cardinals, Texas Rangers and Arizona Diamondbacks.

Standing on the pitcher's mound during the National League Championship Series; it was the first inning with one out. Runners were on first and third when the premier power hitter of the year walked up to the plate. The walls of the stadium began closing in on the young pitcher. He took a deep breath and remembered the words of his performance coach, "Trust the system, Todd. Just trust the system."

Years later and after earning three World Series rings, he is now staring down investment bankers at an elite Wall Street firm. Suddenly, he's back in the spotlight but this time he's swimming with the sharks of Wall Street. The familiar walls are closing in and his saving grace once again is to fall back on his trusted system for achieving monumental success.

The achievement system in this book, influenced by

elite performance coaches, will even out the playing field in your pursuit of excellence.

In *Relentless Success*, Todd reflects on growing up in Yankee Stadium with Mickey Mantle and how these legends shaped his life. By exploring these life lessons along with Todd's 9-point success system, this book will equip you to approach major league results.

To connect with Todd go to: ToddStottlemyre.com